S mon Wilde has been the cricket correspondent of the *Sunday
nes* since 1998. He is the author of numerous books, three of
ich have been shortlisted for the William Hill Sports Book
he Year prize. Most recently, he ghosted David Gower's
noir, *An Endangered Species,* and was the author of *Ian
ham: The Power and the Glory,* both of which were also
lished by Simon & Schuster. He lives in Hampshire.

Also by Simon Wilde

Ian Botham: The Power and the Glory

ON
PIETERSEN

SIMON WILDE

**SIMON &
SCHUSTER**

London · New York · Sydney · Toronto · New Delhi

A CBS COMPANY

First published in Great Britain by Simon & Schuster UK Ltd, 2014
This paperback edition published by Simon & Schuster UK Ltd, 2015
A CBS COMPANY

1 3 5 7 9 10 8 6 4 2

Simon & Schuster UK Ltd
1st Floor
222 Gray's Inn Road
London WC1X 8HB

www.simonandschuster.co.uk

Simon & Schuster Australia, Sydney
Simon & Schuster India, New Delhi

A CIP catalogue copy for this book
is availablefrom the British Library.

ISBN: 978-1-47113-819-5
eBook ISBN: 978-1-47113-820-1

Typeset in the UK by M Rules
Printed and bound by CPI Group (UK) Ltd, Croydon, CR0 4YY

THE CIRCLE OF LIFE

'In effect, South African cricket threw me out. Under the quota system, every state side had to include four players of colour. Three years ago, they [Natal] signed a coloured player who, like me, bowled spin. I knew that Natal would not play two spinners, so the coloured player would always have an advantage, regardless of ability. I firmly believe teams should be selected on merit alone and I was faced with a situation where my opportunities would be limited for other reasons.'

Kevin Pietersen, quoted in the Independent, *21 July 2003*

'The England team needs to rebuild after the whitewash in Australia. To do that we must invest in our captain Alastair Cook and we must support him in creating a culture in which we can be confident he will have the full support of all players, with everyone pulling in the same direction and able to trust each other. It is for those reasons that we have decided to move on without Kevin Pietersen.'

ECB statement on the sacking of Kevin Pietersen,
9 February 2014

CONTENTS

INTRODUCTION

FOR ANYONE whose job it was to report on the England cricket team, Kevin Pietersen was the gift that just kept on giving. He rarely did anything that was dull. He played some of the greatest innings seen by a man in an England shirt and even when he was struggling, as occasionally happened, he did it in interesting ways. Who would have thought he could have got into such a tangle against run-of-the-mill left-arm spinners? But it was not just what happened on the field that was eventful: he had a habit, which he never quite kicked, of saying, doing (or even once whistling) the wrong thing. As Michael Vaughan once observed, his lips did not work quite as well as his bat. Of course, this only added to the fun of the journalistic fair.

Pietersen himself saw it rather differently: he soon wearied of the trouble, much of which he felt was unwarranted and due to media mischief. In his last couple of years as an England player, he had as little to do with us in the press box as he could. He preferred to speak with allies in radio or television. He blocked us on Twitter. In return, he was held by some in little affection.

Once the 2013-14 tour of Australia started to go badly, it seemed more likely that Pietersen and England would go their separate ways: either he would walk off into a Twenty20-tinted sunset or Andy Flower would make the case for rebuilding the team without him. When the axing came, though, it was still a depressing moment. Those of us who have spent years watching cricket for a living are pretty hard to impress, but there are a few players who demand attention and Pietersen was certainly one, along with Brian Lara, Shane Warne and Sachin Tendulkar (if only because you knew one billion others were watching him as well).

Perhaps England were right on all counts; maybe he was too much trouble and maybe there were no more great innings left in him. Maybe from his point of view, being sacked was a good career move on the basis that it left people wanting more. But England should be grateful for the good times: the Pietersen era brought them much success and but for him a lot of it would not have happened. It's going to be dull without him.

1

PIETERSEN AND IDENTITY

THE MYERS-BRIGGS Type Indicator is not something you hear much about in sporting circles, but in the increasingly scientific world of professional cricket it is one of many measures the English game has used to profile elite athletes. In essence, it is a means of psychological profiling, or a personality test, and is commonly used in business, the armed services and government to help workers define their roles and develop team-work. In a team sport the aim is the same: to work out how divergent personalities might best blend into a smooth-running unit. Based on the theories of the Swiss psychiatrist Carl Jung, the test typically requires the respondent to answer more than 80 questions posing one of two possible answers. Based on their responses, four elements of their personality are determined – extraversion/introversion, sensing/intuition, thinking/feeling and judging/

perception – and they are allocated one of 16 four-letter 'types'.

So complex and contradictory is his character that psychologically profiling Kevin Pietersen might be something a lot of us might be keen to do. What on earth would the Myers-Briggs test tell us? Well, we don't need to speculate too much because Pietersen let slip some of its findings during one of the more revealing interviews he gave.

Pietersen's exchanges with the media could be frustrating affairs. Sometimes he just didn't want to be there and offered nothing. At other times, generally when there was a TV camera present and there was an element of 'live' performance, he could be forthcoming and entertaining. In the build-up to the Ashes series in England in 2013, he agreed to an interview with BBC Radio; no doubt it helped that the man conducting the interview was a former team-mate, Andrew Flintoff, even if he and Flintoff had not always been bosom-buddies in the dressing-room because of their comparable superstar status. There was still an edginess, but with with Flintoff safely in retirement, Pietersen saw a kindred spirit; a man who knew something of what he went through in his daily existence. In these circumstances, he trusted Flintoff and trust – or the absence of it – was always a good starting point when it came to Pietersen and relationships.

Asked how he had felt when he first joined the England dressing-room as a one-day player in the winter of 2004-05, Pietersen replied: 'I was scared … Coming into any environment I think anybody's scared, anybody's nervous. I was certainly scared.' He added: 'I'm still scared ... even in circumstances that I'm not comfortable now. I've got this reputation of being confident and stuff, yet you go and do all these psychology tests, all these Myers-Briggs tests, and I'm an introvert. I'm very much an introverted person. I like my own company, I like my own family. I don't really go out ... The confidence has grown from what I've achieved on the cricket field, but I'm not as confident as anybody thinks.'

At first glance, the idea that Pietersen might be scared of anything is extraordinary. He seems – has always seemed – one of the most confident people on the planet. That he describes himself as an introvert is surprising; with a bat in his hand, Pietersen appears to have few self-doubts and often little respect for even the finest bowlers. Fearlessness is a hallmark of his game. Most sportsmen are afraid of failing; it is what drives them on. Not him; at least not in the day-to-day business of batting. He confirmed this during a masterclass he gave for Sky TV a few weeks after the Flintoff interview, repeating something he said many times when discussing the risks he took: 'I've never been scared to get out.' It was pretty evident from the way he batted that this was the case. So if he feared something, it wasn't the individual death of a dismissal.

I would suggest that fear – specifically the fear of rejection – was actually a big part of Pietersen's story. Determined to achieve sporting success from an early stage, certainly earlier than anyone else saw it for him, he set himself on a difficult course. Few high-flyers get to the top without experiencing bumps along the way, but Pietersen's path was highly uncon-ventional and awkward. Certainly it was not a path that could have sat easily with a middle-class boy from Pietermaritzburg, an hour's drive inland from Durban and a place outsiders liked to disparage as having less life than a graveyard.

His mother was English, his father a God-fearing Dutch-born Afrikaner who demanded discipline and conformity of his four sons. Sunday mass was a ritual and one of Kevin's two elder brothers, Tony, became a church minister. Pietersen barely drank and lived a clean life. They were a close-knit family but not especially well off, and Pietersen attended Maritzburg College, renowned for producing good white sportsmen, only as a day-boy. He said he developed his fighting spirit as a survival mechanism because he was one of four boys. 'We all hated losing, whatever we did. We couldn't even jump in the swim-ming pool without saying, "Let's have a race".' Another time he said: 'They [his brothers] battered me. I learned self-belief and how to survive.' He wasn't unfamiliar with being caned. He sold his conformity dear, as he always would.

The discipline of his other older brother, Gregg, who swam competitively in his youth, set an early example as to how to approach sport. Kevin was himself a good swimmer, good rugby player and became an obsessive, often solitary, fitness trainer, setting himself to beat all his peers. This became almost an end in itself.

Pietersen's decision to leave South Africa for a career in English cricket is one of the best-known facts about him. It was, after all, the defining act of his life. Without it, he would never have been the cricketer he became, and would never have attracted the publicity that has rarely left his side since. What is less well chronicled is the early heartache that the move brought him and the extent to which his early struggle for acceptance shaped his personality.

The few weeks he spent playing club cricket in England in 2000, and the English summers that followed at Nottinghamshire, put him in precisely the kind of unfamiliar environments that he told Flintoff made him feel most awkward. At one point he was sufficiently homesick that his parents flew over to support him. But if he was to convince people of his worth as a cricketer, he had little choice but to clear these emotional hurdles.

In Nottingham, his first billet was a bed and breakfast. 'It was very difficult at first,' he recalled in an interview with the *Sunday Times* in 2005. 'I was told that practice would be at ten o'clock next morning and I remember jumping in the car and driving around Nottingham and getting lost trying to find things. I was a young South African kid who didn't know what to expect, chucked into a house with a lady I didn't know. I was a long way from my family and couldn't talk to anyone about anything. I'd go to bed by myself and my head would just spin. "What's tomorrow going to bring?" I thought, "I have to make a success of this. There is no going back." Adapt or die.'

Perhaps only Pietersen still believes that he left South Africa solely because he was disillusioned with the quota system that insisted each provincial team had to include several cricketers of colour. It was a controversial system, it was not popular with many people in the game, and it was eventually abandoned, but nor can it be purely blamed for Pietersen's inability to break into the KwaZulu-Natal side.

The tipping point – according to Pietersen's version of events – came when the KwaZulu-Natal selectors chose Gulam Bodi, of Indian extraction and like Pietersen a batsman who bowled spin, ahead of him. Pietersen was aggrieved and responded to the decision by petulantly throwing a water-bottle across the dressing-room. Dennis Carlstein, who was present, said: 'Kevin was upset and moaned a lot. He was never one for hiding his feelings. In that way, he was quite immature.'

Pietersen, aged 20, phoned his father in tears. He was angry because he knew – *knew* – that Gulam wasn't as good as him, but this was not a view shared by many within KwaZulu-Natal cricket. Bodi was a good all-rounder who, in the months after Pietersen walked away, scored his maiden first-class century and took a career-best six for 63. A few months later he was called up by South Africa as a replacement on a tour of West Indies (unfortunately he was injured before departure). In 2007 Bodi was included in South Africa's World Twenty20 squad. Pietersen obviously went on to much greater things, but back in 2000-01 Bodi's preferment was far from the travesty it was sometimes presented as.

The crucial point was that at the time Pietersen quit KwaZulu-Natal he had already received an offer to play for Nottinghamshire through their director of cricket Clive Rice, himself a South African and a man contemptuous of the way politics had taken over cricket in his country (Pietersen's grumbles about quotas were largely a parroting of Rice's views). Pietersen's original terms of a three-year contract were incredibly generous given that Rice had seen little of Pietersen and was acting on no more than a hunch that he could cope in English conditions. Rice had heard of Pietersen's heavy run-scoring for Cannock in the Birmingham and District Premier League, an assignment Pietersen had got by chance only after a first-choice signing pulled out.

Rice's instinct proved accurate but he took a huge gamble which few other county coaches would have dared take. Thus, when Pietersen sought various assurances about his future from KwaZulu-Natal officials and even from Ali Bacher, the then head of South African cricket, he was doing so from a position of some strength. Unsurprisingly, they were unwilling to back this near-nonentity to the same extent as Rice; indeed, in financial terms, it would have been very difficult for them to do so. Pietersen was paid £15,000 in his first year at Trent Bridge, almost four times the value of the junior contract that KwaZulu-Natal put under his nose as their best offer. Graham Ford, South Africa's national coach at the time and a family friend whom the Pietersens consulted as to Kevin's best way forward, said later that the choice was a 'no-brainer': he had to choose Nottinghamshire.

It was not a risk-free deal though. Thanks to the British passport he owned through his mother, Pietersen would be able to play in England as a local rather than as the one designated overseas player each county was allowed – this was part of the attraction of the arrangement to Rice – but he could no longer play in South Africa as a local as well. He could pursue a career in one place or the other, but not both. It was actually a wider rule governing cricket – that no player could appear as a local in two countries concurrently – that therefore determined the course of Pietersen's career, rather than South Africa's quota system.

Rice's offer may have been one he could not turn down, but that did not make the move to England to start a new life any easier for a young man whose existence to that point had been pretty sheltered. All the indications are that he was far from comfortable at the prospect of emigrating. Convincing himself that he had no choice – that South Africa had in effect rejected him – may have smoothed the bitter pill. 'In his own mind, his country had let him down,' Peter Roebuck wrote of Pietersen in 2008. 'Of course it was an over-simplification, but it has been a powerful motivating force.'

Only after his successes began piling up for Nottinghamshire did his statements about one day playing for England – for whom he could qualify after four years of residence – grow more assured. He admitted in his interview with Flintoff that when he first came over he was trying to pursue a dream of playing professional sport, not international sport, and at the end of his first season at Nottinghamshire he had a business card made up: 'Kevin Pietersen: Professional Cricketer.' On one level his talk about playing for England might have sounded presumptuous – it *did* sound presumptuous – but on another it bound him to live up to his big words. He had to rise, or face ridicule. Adapt or die.

*

PIETERSEN often gave the impression that he did not care whether he was liked, but this was not the case. He did not always endear himself to people by speaking his mind with a bluntness that left Englishmen uneasy, and by his own admission he was not easy to get to know at this stage (was he ever?), but he certainly came to England eager for acceptance. Yet he got the opposite: downright hostility. This probably had less to do with him (although a three-year contract on the back of negligible evidence can't have helped) and more to do with where he came from. Home-grown English players had grown weary of foreigners, especially South Africans, and especially those armed with British passports, coming over and taking up positions that could be filled by locals. And so the Nottinghamshire players made Pietersen stand up in the dressing-room with Australian leg-spinner Stuart MacGill, the club's overseas player, and sing the words to the British national anthem, something Pietersen managed without difficulty, much to their surprise. Pietersen said the team put him through other 'tests' too, while those opponents hurling abuse certainly did not wait to find out whether they liked him as a bloke. Such a climate was hardly conducive to developing friendships.

Pietersen admitted to being shocked at the level of hostility. 'As a kid I had always supported England because it is where my mother is from,' he said in a newspaper interview shortly before he made his England debut in 2004. 'My hero was Rob Andrew and during the 1995 World Cup in South Africa I used to wear an England rugby shirt. I copped a lot of flak for this, but nothing like the flak I received when I first arrived here [England]. Wherever I played I was being abused for being a South African. Opponents would say that they had never met a decent South African and that I wasn't good enough and they accused me of coming over here and stealing their money. My first game in England was a friendly against Derbyshire, and we all know what Dominic Cork is like when he starts to carry on. I used to walk out to bat, knowing I was on my own.'

In another interview at around the same time, he said there had been occasions when he wondered whether it might have been easier to return home. Nor was the antipathy confined to the cricketers; the wider public was also increasingly sceptical at the number of imports playing under flags of convenience.

Two things emerged. One was that Pietersen realised that if he was not to return to South Africa a beaten man, he had to create the right mentality: unless he believed in himself, no one else was going to. Flying halfway round the world to a B&B in Nottingham had taught him that. Any doubts as to whether he was good enough were buried deep within himself, never to resurface. 'Confidence in sport is everything,' was a phrase never far from his lips. He created what was almost an alter ego: a brash exterior topped off with a line in haircuts whose exoticism marched in step with the growing flamboyance of his stroke-play. The nearer he got to the controversy of a debut for his adopted country, the more outlandish his appearance became. Afraid? How could he be when he had the nerve to dress so outrageously? No wonder Ed Smith, years later, called him a 'genius of self-belief'.

The second thing he must have noticed was that when he got

into controversy – as he had simply by leaving South Africa in the way that he did – it brought out the best in him. He may well have been scared when he found himself in uncomfortable situations, but it transpired that those uncomfortable situations could produce the sort of creative tension on which he thrived. 'He is at his most vulnerable when he has succeeded in proving himself,' Andrew Strauss, who captained Pietersen in 46 of his 104 Tests, wrote in 2013. 'If he is happy and comfortable, away from the limelight, he starts to resemble lesser mortals … Pietersen's history – moving from South Africa, frequently changing teams and a willingness to court controversy – suggests he knows this. If he has nothing to prove then he loses his edge.'

So, if creative tension was good for him, why worry if that tension arose in the first place? It became a vindication of itself: he could behave as he liked because even if he upset people there was always a good chance of redeeming himself. After a very public parting of the ways with Nottinghamshire in 2004, Pietersen had no trouble backing up his assertion that he needed to leave because he was no longer progressing; his game immediately went up another level. Many of his most brilliant performances came when he was most troubled, or most troublesome, as evidenced by his astonishing century at Headingley in 2012 at the time of his falling-out with the England dressing-room.

Even so, it must have been a lonely, scary path in those early days: Pietersen alone with his dreams, taking on a sceptical world. Had he any real concept of his place in it? Was he South African or English? Was he really this brash, confident, hard-working youngster bashing people's ears as to how good he was, or was he the polite, respectful boy who lowered his eyes while the family said grace before meals, and was nervous of what his peers really thought of him? Rather than ever being answered, these confusing thoughts also got buried deep beneath the surface of a personality that acquired any number of baroque ornamentations as his achievements on the cricket field grew – the diamond ear-rings and the tattoos, as well as the various manifestations of dyed hair. 'Anyone that arrives with blue hair has got to be able to play a bit,' said Michael Vaughan, Pietersen's first England captain. 'To be able to create that external image and then play to the standard which he did takes some doing.'

It is hardly surprising, given the circumstances, that Pietersen proved better at solving problems in his own area of expertise – batting – than at inter-personal relationships. As he said, he is an introvert. The Myers-Briggs Type Indicator defines the introvert as someone who acts only after reflecting, and who needs to rebuild their energy through quiet time alone, away from activity. Although he was often castigated for choosing the wrong shot at the wrong time, Pietersen's success was based on a careful study of batting, a study that led him frequently to take calculated risks – often very successfully – and devise new strokes to deal with particular problems. Everything was underpinned by sound principles. Having thought through the consequences, he was not afraid to tear up coaching convention if he concluded it was the best thing to do: only someone who had given the matter a great deal of thought could have batted as unorthodoxly but as productively as he did. While many of his public pronouncements appeared clumsy and misjudged, he could speak with great clarity and intelligence on the science of batsmanship. It was, after all, a subject he knew inside out. He had an analytical mind and sought depth of knowledge rather than breadth of knowledge. All this categorises him as an introvert according to Myers-Briggs.

So much peripheral stuff was attached to his life – the celebrity, the controversies, the dramas – that it was easy to overlook his passion and obsession for his craft. He was often asked what motivated him, and his standard reply was that he was driven to get up every day to try and improve. Fielding and physical drills could be a bore, he conceded, but scoring runs – well, that was something he just wanted to keep on doing. Vaughan was immediately struck by the thoroughness of Pietersen's approach when he joined England. 'He trained harder than any other England player and [had] this kind of professional nature of looking at the opposition. He really analysed the kind of bowlers that we were going to be facing and the kind of shots that he was going to be requiring to play well against them.' He was a batting junkie.

It cannot have been easy when simple talent created a gulf between him and his colleagues. Certainly he sometimes found it hard to comprehend why others could not do what he did. 'We would be sat on the balcony during our innings and Kevin would be saying, "He should have pulled that ball," or "He should have driven that ball",' said Jason Gallian, who captained Pietersen at Nottinghamshire (and spectacularly fell out with him). 'It would frustrate him and he would be more than happy to tell you what the batsman should be doing. He expected other people to be able to do what he could do, which is sometimes impossible.'

After scoring a rapid 61 that almost took Hampshire to victory in his first Championship match for them, he walked back into the visitors' dressing-room at Hove, took off his pads and sat down between Alan Mullally and Shane Warne. He said: 'Hey Al, I'm pretty good, aren't I?' Was this a remark prompted by sheer big-headedness or a desire for acceptance? Mullally was in no doubt: 'Kev had his insecurities, perhaps about not being born in this country, and he overcame that with arrogance and brashness ... I can remember thinking at the time it was just him wanting to be loved, and being insecure.'

Mullally told his new team-mate to 'pull his head in', but a few weeks later Pietersen behaved in almost identical fashion after scoring a lustrous 91 off just 65 balls to take England to victory over Australia in a one-day international at Bristol. On that occasion he returned to the dressing-room to announce: 'Not bad, am I?' No doubt his England team-mates were grateful for the victory he had just delivered, but this was hardly a comment likely to endear him to a group still coming to terms with this new phenomenon in their midst.

By no stretch could Pietersen have been called a collectivist. He did not need interaction in the way many people do and this may have set him further at odds with the typical mood of a dressing-room. As he said to Flintoff: 'I like my own company, I like my own family. I don't really go out ...'

He also told Flintoff that when he batted, he had to focus on his own game completely if it was to function properly. 'From my side, when I bat, I have to solely concentrate on what I'm doing to get my batting right,' he said. 'Then I'll do whatever I can to help the other batter to make him more composed.' This account was confirmed by Geraint Jones's anecdote about a mid-pitch exchange he had with Pietersen when they were batting together: 'Can't talk now, buddy ... Too pumped.'

It is one of cricket's charms that it can accommodate diverse personalities and it would be wrong to condemn someone who doesn't conform to the norm as a dangerous maverick or selfishly wrapped up in his own concerns. Was it wrong that Pietersen wanted to drive a different sponsored car, or wear different sponsored shoes, from the standard ones offered to England players? Was he undermining the team ethic or was it a reasonable request from a man wanting to express his individuality?

Doubtful of being able to gain acceptance by conventional means, Pietersen perhaps sought approval by other avenues: by getting the Three Lions tattooed on his left bicep, by acquiring celebrity friends, building up more than 1.75 million Twitter followers, and earning more money than anyone else in English cricket. It was as though he was saying not 'That's how good I am,' but 'That's how much someone loves me.'

To Vaughan, love was the key with Pietersen: 'He needs a little bit of an arm round him. These superstars ... those with all the lyrics, generally aren't as confident as their lyrics would suggest they are. Kev's no different to that. You need to manage these guys. You need to love them.' Much was made of Pietersen's marriage to Jessica Taylor, a pop star with the band Liberty X, but he was insistent that they had little interest in living up to the tabloids' wish for them to be the Posh 'n' Becks of cricket. He described Jessica as a 'very shy girl' and they declined to sell photographs of their wedding in December 2007. 'We're not interested in all the nonsense,' he said. 'People say I'm a showman and that I like flashy things ... No. I like being successful.'

Surely only a lack of confidence can explain why, when Pietersen was promoting his first autobiography in the summer of 2006, he chose to take along with him to a book-signing session in London his agent, his parents, two brothers and a sister-in-law. 'He looks over at his entourage at least six times a minute, like a boy in a nativity play,' noted Rachel Cooke in the *Observer*.

Relationships tended to hit trouble when Pietersen could not see love, only a grievance. He believed he was wrongly man-oeuvred out of the England captaincy after voicing doubts about the coaching style of Peter Moores, doubts that some senior players appeared to share. When he lobbied the ECB and England team management in 2012 to be allowed more time to play in the Indian Premier League – he had just signed a deal for $2 million with Delhi Daredevils which depended on him playing a full season to get all the money – he felt he was engaged in a battle that needed fighting, and not just for himself. They declined to accommodate him.

He was also upset in both instances – with the talks over his relationship with Moores and talks over his England contract – that details reached the press. With the contract situation still rumbling on in the summer of 2012, he was stung that a lampooning Twitter account turned out to have been created by a friend of Stuart Broad's and was being followed by several England players. 'It's tough being me in this dressing-room,' he famously said.

It was with that problem at its height that he lurched into one of his most catastrophic errors – there were a few – by sending text messages to South Africa opposition players apparently complaining about his captain Andrew Strauss. Pietersen had sometimes appeared happier mixing with opponents than his own team and he had got to know some of the South Africans during the IPL. He once described Australians as his favourite people because they shared his outlook on life. The South Africans and Pietersen insisted the text messages were merely banter, but once they came to light it was inevitable he would be disciplined. Strauss later wrote that the text affair was caused by the IPL and Pietersen 'falling out of love with the England team environment'; he said Pietersen had 'felt unloved and uncared for'. Whether or not Pietersen was justified in those feelings, it was revealing that that was his state of mind; so much for the teak-hard self-confidence.

Although Pietersen was soon recalled – under new captain Alastair Cook, Strauss having retired – it was always going to be difficult to repair relations with the other senior players and Andy Flower, the team director. Strauss said that a chasm had been opened up between them. When Pietersen was deemed to have transgressed again during the catastrophic Ashes tour of 2013-14, he found that neither Flower, Cook nor – apparently – the senior players were prepared to come to his defence. This time he was not disciplined but sacked altogether from the team.

'We must support him [Cook] in creating a culture in which we can be confident he will have the full support of all players, with everyone pulling in the same direction and able to trust each other,' an ECB statement read. Pietersen took the news badly, allegedly cutting short a meeting with Cook and Paul Downton, the managing director of England cricket, before the reasons could be fully explained. The following day Pietersen posted on Twitter a picture of himself leaving the field at Sydney in the final Ashes Test of the winter: 'So sad that this will now be the last time I leave a field in an England shirt ... incredibly.'

Why couldn't Pietersen rub along with people better? Why did his lips not work as well as his bat? It seemed baffling that he could not think more carefully before he spoke or display more diplomacy. Iain O'Brien, a recently retired New Zealand Test player, offered an interesting view on the Cricinfo website shortly after the text scandal. He suggested that dysfunctional dressing-room relationships were not that uncommon and that he himself had sometimes behaved in an aloof and detached manner, not because that was how he really was but because he feared the judgement of his peers: You like me don't you? I am pretty good, aren't I?

'There is a very easy image to conjure of an arrogant sportsman: sunglasses on, chest out, tattoos, and a "you can't touch me" strut ... Is that really what's going on behind the lenses? Behind my sunglasses I was always analysing ... You can just analyse, be uncomfortable but safe in your own little world. As long as I knew what people thought of me – like me or not – I was more comfortable ... Subconsciously you'd turn people against you, so at least you could control one part of the relationship. There are so many who just don't know how to handle themselves around their sport. They are good enough to play, and play for a long time. Some even get the Three Lions tattooed on themselves and strut around with egos, sometimes acting like they are bigger than the game. Or are they? Is there more to it than the simplistic "arrogant knob" label? Is it self-confidence? Is it pure arrogance? Or is it the exact opposite – a lack of self-confidence, a bluff, an "I just want to be liked but don't know how to get people to like me"?' O'Brien knew what it was like to feel that life was tough 'being me'.

Perhaps by the time of the ill-fated winter of 2013-14, Pietersen was simply tired of the battle for acceptance, tired of the pretending. Perhaps he had always known, deep down, that what he had done, by turning his back on South Africa and pledging allegiance to England, was irreconcilable and would end, ultimately, in betrayal. The beginning of his story foretold the end.

2

PIETERSEN AS SAVIOUR

PIETERSEN COULD be forgiven for thinking he was important. After all, England were very keen to have him. In fact, they couldn't wait to get him in their side. They picked him for an A team tour two years into his four-year qualification and even named him for his first full England tour – a one-day tour of Zimbabwe – before that period was up. He officially became eligible for selection for England on 27 October 2004 and took the field for the first time in an international at Harare Sports Club on 28 November. There was a delay in him receiving his first shirt as the makers originally mis-spelt his name 'Pieterson'. It didn't happen again.

The previous year, when Pietersen's consistently brilliant performances for Nottinghamshire made it apparent that the matter was going to be of relevance, exactly when his residential qualification would be complete was the cause of some confusion. The regulations demanded that a person seeking to qualify should reside in the country for 210 days a year for four straight years, but logging such attendance was rarely easy. Asked for clarification by a newspaper reporter in July 2003, the ECB stated, 'Standard practice would be for Pietersen to qualify from the start of an English season, in this case 2005. But the registration committee could consider an appeal for him to be available immediately after the end of next season.' In the event, he was deemed free to play for England from the earlier date.

England needed players like Pietersen. There was no sure way of knowing if he would be good enough for the top level until he was tried, but if he was he was plainly going to play the sort of attacking game that few other batsmen in the country could provide. At the time that Pietersen started his county career, England's Test team was only just starting to shake off years of mediocrity. The 1990s had been a bleak decade. The country simply could not produce enough good bowlers, or keep fit those that were good enough, to assemble a potent attack, while many of their opponents were armed with some of the greatest bowlers of all time. West Indies had Courtney Walsh and Curtly Ambrose, South Africa Allan Donald and Shaun Pollock, Pakistan Wasim Akram and Waqar Younis and Australia Shane Warne and Glenn McGrath. Unsurprisingly England's batsmen struggled to cope.

Things started to improve once Nasser Hussain and Duncan Fletcher teamed up as captain and coach in 1999 and central contracts were introduced. West Indies were beaten in a series for the first time in 31 years and two series were won in Asia in the winter of 2000-01, but there was still no toppling the Australian ziggurat. Pietersen's first summer at Nottinghamshire coincided with England losing a home Ashes series 4-1; 18 months later in 2002-03 the result was replicated Down Under, England's eighth straight Ashes series defeat. The problems posed by Warne and McGrath seemed insuperable. World Cups had also become routine exercises in English humiliation: all the flair and firepower that other leading sides seemed to possess in abundance was all too evidently missing from their game.

When Michael Vaughan replaced Hussain as Test captain in July 2003, he and Fletcher began plotting for the 2005 Ashes. In Vaughan's first series, South Africa were held to a 2-2 draw, a score-line that flattered England somewhat, but then in 2004 the components fell into place for a menacing four-man pace attack of Steve Harmison, Andrew Flintoff, Simon Jones and Matthew Hoggard. That year England played 13 Tests and won 11.

That left the main problem a creaking middle order, with the clock running down on the careers of Hussain, Mark Butcher and Graham Thorpe. Ian Bell was seen as a great batsman in the making but he was young and, like many English cricketers of his age, diffident and unsure how to impose himself on international bowlers. Australia, past masters at bullying opponents and especially England, weren't going to be frightened of Bell and he could form only a part of the answer. Vaughan and Fletcher were on the look-out for people who weren't going to take a backward step. On the face of it, Nottinghamshire's swaggering 6ft 4in batsman appeared to fit the blueprint.

Pietersen did well in Zimbabwe, scoring 104 runs for once out, and when Flintoff was withdrawn with an injury from a seven-match one-day series in South Africa it presented the perfect excuse to get Pietersen back in the team (Fletcher said Pietersen would have been added to the squad anyway after how he had played in Zimbabwe). Pietersen was originally spared selection for South Africa on the grounds that it might heap too much pressure on him, asking him to return to his homeland so soon. Vaughan and Fletcher, having got to know him better, now reckoned he was worth the risk. He did brilliantly, scoring three hundreds, one of them off 69 balls, the fastest for England in any one-day international. Back in England he played equally breathtakingly to win a one-day match against Australia in Bristol – the time he went back into the dressing-room and declared, 'Not bad, am I?'

'He played well straight away,' Vaughan recalled. 'Some of those knocks in that one-day series in South Africa were quite incredible. We played poorly as a team. He stood out hugely as an individual. Then we got to 2005. For two years we'd been planning to arrive in this [Ashes] series with a different mindset and a different set of players, younger players with no baggage from the past and a fearless and aggressive approach. I saw the way Pietersen had played in those one-dayers [against South Africa] and after the first century I walked up to Fletch and said he's got to play in the Ashes. He's perfect to take on Warne and McGrath, who had been our nemesis for so many series. They were the two we had to try to play a little bit better, at least more positively and score off them.' Vaughan and

Fletcher saw Pietersen as the man that could do that. They dumped Thorpe, a veteran of 100 Tests, and brought him in. England had played seven Tests since Pietersen became eligible for selection. Over the next nine years, he would never again be left out of the Test team on grounds of merit.

ANY SPORTS team that is used to regular troughs in form will be familiar with the concept of the Saviour, one man who at a stroke can sort all the ills and deliver on the greatest wishes. Ian Botham did much to keep the idea prominent in English cricket mythology by turning an Ashes series on its head in 1981, but for sheer potency it was hard to beat the Saviour who arrived only after a prolonged period of waiting and anticipation.

Of course, not every proclaimed Saviour lives up to the billing. Few cricketers made a more eagerly anticipated England debut than the Zimbabwe-born Graeme Hick, who spent seven years qualifying under the rules in place during his time. Five years into his seven-year wait, questions were raised by an intrepid journalist at *The Times* – me, actually – as to whether he had actually fulfilled the 210-days-a-year rule, but a specially convened meeting of the Test and County Cricket Board (as the ECB then was) decided all was in order. England had reason to be even more keen to get Hick on board in 1991 than they would be later to acquire Pietersen; since triumphing in Australia in 1986-87 they had won only two series in nine.

It turned out the Saviour's feet were made of clay. Hick spent his qualification period pulverising county attacks, but he was a tall man with a front-foot game whose methods proved ill-suited to international cricket, where he was peppered with precisely targeted short-pitched bowling. Temperamentally, too, he was unsuited to withstand the aggression of opponents intent on not letting him settle in the Test arena; confrontation was simply not part of his nature. He came and went for ten years before England dropped him once and for all in 2001, so his case was still relatively fresh in everyone's mind at the time Pietersen prepared to make his entrance.

When Hick first set his sights on playing for England, his native country of Zimbabwe did not have Test match status, so his decision to settle in England was received with a fair amount of sympathy. He was a fine player and deserved the chance to test himself at the highest level. Even so, as a character he inspired little warmth among English cricket supporters, especially as he repeatedly flattered to deceive. Those who had been so keen to recruit him were left looking grubbily expedient. Hick spent 25 years in England, but after retiring emigrated to Australia. There were echoes of the case in the mid-1980s of Zola Budd, a South African middle-distance runner who was brought to England by the *Daily Mail* in order that she could circumvent an anti-apartheid sports ban and run for Britain instead. Her career for her second home failed to meet expectations and proved short lived.

By the time Pietersen was closing in on an England cap, people were not so easily fooled by sports men and women declaring undying love for their adopted country. County cricket was awash with foreigners, many of them South

Africans, who happened to own a British passport through their ancestors, playing as 'locals'; in May 2003 the Kolpak ruling, which granted workers from countries with trade agreements with the European Union the same rights as an EU worker, opened the door further to overseas cricketers. For many of them, their aspirations stopped at finding regular employment with a county. Others simply used county cricket as a training ground before returning home. In the mid-1990s Andrew Symonds, who had learnt his cricket in Australia but had been born in England, professed an ambition to play for England, spent a few seasons in county cricket playing as a 'local', only to switch allegiance back to Australia when they were ready to pick him. He was, it transpired, a 'fair dinkum Aussie' after all. Cynicism was rife.

To his credit, Pietersen was ready for the fuss that surrounded his qualification, certainly much more so than Hick had been. He was 24 years of age when he first played for England, a year younger than Hick when he became eligible, and coped with the pressure and expectation much more easily. Like Hick he was a big man, which potentially meant problems against the short ball, but he was a more confident person, and smarter too. He was eager to solve any problems that might arise. He knew he would be under pressure when he entered Test cricket and knew he would be targeted in the same way Hick had been, all the more so because of how Hick buckled under the onslaught. But he could see the advantages to the position he was in.

Interviewed shortly before leaving for his first England tour, he told the *Daily Mail*: 'When Graeme Hick qualified for England, the team weren't doing as well as they are now and he was seen as the saviour. For the last three years so many people have said, "There's so much pressure on you." But that's not the case. England are doing well and it's a matter of trying to break into the team. I'm not being seen as a saviour. It's a fantastic position to be in. There is pressure to perform because of what I have achieved but I just have to knuckle down and not worry about it. It's easier to come into a winning team anyway.'

What was not easier was the general hostility directed towards him almost from the day he arrived at Trent Bridge. This was not confined to the home-grown players on the county circuit. The media were also on the offensive. Pietersen had not yet completed his first month with Nottinghamshire when David Lloyd, who had coached England from 1996 to 1999 and was now a Sky TV pundit, criticised counties for scouring the world for flag-of-convenience players holding EC passports. Nottinghamshire's coach Clive Rice defended his signing as a *bona fide* British citizen. 'I wonder if these whingers will change their tune when Pietersen is in the England side after qualifying for selection ... He's come here to make a commitment to English cricket and he's in our side [at Nottinghamshire] because he's the best player available to do the job.' Lloyd resumed his attack when the possibility of Pietersen leaving Notts surfaced two years later, saying on television that his next move should be to Western Province in Cape Town. Pietersen heard the remark and laughed.

Christopher Martin-Jenkins, writing in *The Times* towards

the end of Pietersen's first season, saw a parallel with the career of Tony Greig, a strikingly tall, blond all-rounder who came over from South Africa in the late 1960s: 'The powerful Kevin Pietersen has . . . made an impact not dissimilar to that of Tony Greig when he first burst on to the English scene at Hove in preparation for a vividly successful Test career as an all-rounder for England. Pietersen, too, has declared his intention to qualify not just for county cricket but for England, a process that will take him four years. There will be those who seek to shorten the period, just as there were with Graeme Hick in the days when a change of nationality took longer. Of Pietersen it will be asked, however, as it was of Greig in John Woodcock's famous phrase, whether he is English through and through.'

Recollections of Greig were awkward for everyone, because after his promotion to the England captaincy in 1975 he 'betrayed' the English game and his post by not only signing up to join Kerry Packer's World Series Cricket but recruiting other English cricketers to join the enterprise. Deemed to have put lucre before loyalty – no matter that cricketers were paid footling amounts at the time – Greig was sacked and never played for England again. There were still those in and around the English game who felt that such behaviour was all that could be expected from people who were not 'English through and through'. The concern was there from the very start: Pietersen might be good enough to play for England, but might he not one day betray them?

Before his fall from grace, Greig was a popular and charismatic figure, but he like Pietersen spoke a little too plainly for

English tastes and landed himself in political hot water for suggesting his England side might make West Indies 'grovel'. Pietersen was no less brash and no less tactlessly arrogant. In England, people preferred to wait for others to tell them how good they were rather than proclaim it themselves. But was all this really any more than the rub of cultural difference? English cricket seemed to want to have it both ways: cherry-pick the best foreign talent, then complain when that talent made decisions based on what was best economically for itself, rather than on an abstract notion of patriotism that simply could not apply to someone born and bred thousands of miles away.

The nearer Pietersen got to playing for England, the higher the temperature of the debate rose. In June 2003, a week after Pietersen had taken a double-century off Warwickshire, Kevin Mitchell wrote in the *Observer*: 'There is a small time bomb ticking in English cricket and his name is Kevin Pietersen . . . Claiming he has been rejected in his own country, he makes no secret of his desire now to play for England . . . You can only assume either that he thought it would be easier to play for England than for South Africa . . . or that, as a professional sportsman, he saw more clout in the pound than the rand. However, while it would be personally satisfying for him, it would be less than ideal for the game if Pietersen were to play for England . . .

'Zola Budd and the *Daily Mail* have a lot to answer for . . . It's not that genuine immigrants shouldn't aspire to represent their new country; that is a desirable aspect of integration and you only have to look at the complexion of any of our national teams to see the lasting benefits of the process. It is different, however, when athletes use a country for their short-term needs.'

Andrew Strauss, who captained Pietersen in more Tests than anyone and ironically was himself the son of South African parents, though he was raised in England from an early age, described Pietersen's relationship with England as having been like 'an illicit affair'.

It was hard for Pietersen to convince his peers of his Englishness given how differently they interpreted things. Nishant Joshi described in *All Out Cricket* in February 2014 how he had attended a two-day academy trial at Trent Bridge in the early 2000s in front of numerous coaches and several Nottinghamshire players. Joshi worked out who Pietersen was from his 'ridiculous, faux-hawk hair'. He said that the best bowler at the trial was a short, chubby Pakistani boy, the youngest triallist in attendance. He had come down from Edinburgh with his father and slept in their car overnight. At first glance it looked like he might provide some easy pickings, but it transpired he could bowl. 'He was ripping leg-spin that was from another planet,' Joshi wrote. 'Flippers, googlies, sliders, all bowled by a kid who was unmistakably out of place. Pietersen took an interest, asking how he gripped it, and then watched with befuddlement as batsmen were castled and lost balance against the spiteful bite that was being extracted. The boy did not make the cut. I overheard Pietersen saying that he had vouched for him vehemently, but the other coaches had vetoed it on account of his lack of fitness. He just *could not understand* how such an obvious talent . . . could be ignored in this country.'

Pietersen took the fuss over his switch of allegiance in his stride, as he had to. There was nothing he could do about the fact that the British media could use his immigrant status against him any time they liked (which was often). As he once told them: 'You guys are always going to make me the bad guy.' And he was capable of making light of the situation, even if they could not. He once quipped to Australia's Ed Cowan in 2010: 'I am not fucking English, Eddie. I am South African. I just work here.' Cowan recorded the conversation in a diary he published and was embarrassed when the anecdote made news in British papers that happily took Pietersen's words at face value. 'He said it as a joke,' Cowan protested. Pietersen, in fact, never showed any signs of wanting to return to South Africa on a permanent basis, marrying an English girl and settling in Chelsea.

Pietersen brought more trouble on himself in respect of the country he had left behind. Perhaps he felt he needed to convince people about his anger over the quota system. Whatever the reason, he said several times he was keen to see South Africa's cricketers 'nailed'; he said the same thing about their rugby players at the 2003 World Cup, which England went on to win. This only assured him of an even more hostile reception when he played in England's one-day series in South Africa in 2004-05. Graeme Smith, the South Africa captain, spoke unflatteringly about him. Pietersen knew, too, what the crowds would be like because he had seen what happened to Clyde

Rathbone, a rugby union wing and former South Africa Under-21 captain who returned to his native Durban to play in a tri-nation for Australia. 'Every single time he touched the ball he was booed,' Pietersen recalled. 'When he ran on to the field he got booed. They absolutely nailed him.'

Even so, the greeting awaiting Pietersen at Johannesburg's Wanderers Stadium took him aback. He fielded first in the circle but Vaughan later dropped him back to the boundary in front of beer-fuelled Afrikaners who let him know precisely what they thought of him. 'It was cut-throat stuff,' he recalled. 'My parents were in shock – my mother was crying when they were swearing and shouting "traitor". People were hysterical.' When he walked out to bat, Vaughan, his partner, noticed the effect the booing had: 'He was shaking. He was clearly shaken up and I could understand why.' Such was the noise that Pietersen and Vaughan could barely hear each other speak and when Pietersen missed his first ball from Andre Nel the crowd went berserk. But urged by Vaughan to watch the ball he survived unbeaten on 22. Pietersen, in fact, quickly came to relish the attention and in his next five innings scored three spectacular hundreds. When he fielded on the boundary in Port Elizabeth and the crowd got after him, he turned and cupped his hand to his ear as though he couldn't hear what was being said. 'As much as he'll say he didn't like it, I think he loved it,' Vaughan said. 'The crowd were all about him.'

Pietersen invited further animosity by continuing to trash South Africa during newspaper interviews in 2005. 'When will he learn that you cannot change the past?' asked columnist

Mark Keohane. 'You cannot wish it away. Kevin, please under-stand that you are not English. You don't speak like them, you don't act like them and you aren't one of them. They'll entertain your dramatics while you're scoring 158 runs to win them the Ashes, but they won't think twice to send you back to county cricket if it all goes to pot in the next eighteen months.'

Pietersen was unperturbed. In an autobiography published in the summer of 2006 he described South Africa's cricket system as 'bullshit', adding: 'It created an artificial team and that will never do anything to encourage the racial integration of cricket in South Africa.' He also described how Smith had had a go at him while he was batting at Johannesburg, the only one of the South Africans to do so. 'I had never met him before, but I thought he was an absolute muppet ... I found his attitude pretty childish. Not many people in world cricket like the man.' Unsurprisingly, Smith responded. 'I'm patriotic and that's why I don't like Kevin Pietersen,' he said. 'The only reason that Kevin and I have never had a relationship is because he slated South Africa. It was his decision to leave and that's fine, but why does he spend so much time slating our country? If he had kept his mouth shut he would have had far fewer people angry at him and taken far less flak.'

It was a fair point and one which Pietersen seemed to take on board; he later toned down his anti-South Africa rhetoric. Smith, for his part, was to experience his own problems with political interference and was ready to resign had he not got his way over the composition of a tour squad in 2008. By the time Smith joined Pietersen at Surrey in 2013, they were happy at the prospect of working together. Smith even took Pietersen's side after England sacked him.

THE BIG difference between Pietersen and Hick was that Pietersen *did* become England's Saviour – and at the very first time of asking. Although Flintoff was officially the man of the series in the 2005 Ashes, it was Pietersen who first took the attack to Warne and McGrath in an opening Test in which Flintoff did little and felt, he later admitted, overawed on his Ashes debut. It was Pietersen who instilled the belief in the team that these goliaths could be slain. With the fate of the series and Ashes in the balance on an agonisingly taut final afternoon at The Oval, it was Pietersen who repulsed the Australian attack. He had done what he had been brought in to do, and ahead of schedule.

Duncan Fletcher, the England coach, had thought that 2005 might be too early for a developing squad to topple Australia, and reckoned 2006-07 might present a better chance (had Australia won in 2005, Warne certainly, and possibly some others, would have retired, improving England's chances thereafter). Within a year of first playing for England, Pietersen delivered the Holy Grail. What is more, so audaciously and entertainingly did he play that even many of those who had doubted his right to play for England were captivated. It did not matter if you were English, South African or Australian: you wanted to watch him and with terrestrial television still holding the broadcast rights to cricket at that stage, a large proportion of the population was in a position to do so.

All this was bound to affect the way Pietersen saw himself. He would not have been human if it hadn't. And what he probably thought was: 'I thought I was important when England were so keen to recruit me. Now I know I am.'

Over the next three years he continued to earn England's gratitude as their best batsman, and when Vaughan resigned in August 2008 his reward was the captaincy. No official England captain since Greig more than 30 years earlier had spent so much of his early life out of the country. The move failed for a variety of reasons but one of the central problems was Pietersen's willingness to speak his mind. His blunt opinion that Peter Moores was not the right person to be head coach was a little too forthright for the tastes of his masters at the ECB, even though it was surely his duty to speak up if that was what he felt. Both captain and coach were swiftly removed and Pietersen's relationship with England never fully recovered. He felt betrayed; the board probably felt he was not, after all, 'one of us'.

England continued to recruit foreigners. In fact the trickle grew to a flood with South Africans, Australians, Irishmen, New Zealanders and Zimbabweans all winning caps, and in 2010 England won the World Twenty20 title in large part thanks to a top three in the batting order of Craig Kieswetter, Michael Lumb and Pietersen, all of whom were born in South Africa. But the mood among the administrators shifted. Legal options were explored and gradually the regulations regarding eligibility for playing in English cricket as a 'local', and playing for England, were tightened. In the spring of 2012, the ECB announced that in future anyone starting residential qualifica-tion for England after their 18th birthday would not be eligible for seven years rather than four. On that basis Pietersen would have had to wait until 2007 and Jonathan Trott, another South African, until 2010, a year after he emulated Pietersen by play-ing an Ashes-deciding innings at The Oval. After Pietersen was sacked in February 2014, board sources said it wanted to restore pride in playing for the country and that 'Englishness' was an important factor in choosing a new head coach in suc-cession to the southern African Andy Flower.

What was easy to forget, though, was that it was in part because he was an outsider with no inhibitions about looking at things afresh that allowed Pietersen to bat in the extraordi-nary and original way that he did.

3

PIETERSEN AS INNOVATOR

PIETERSEN'S whole career has been an expression of individuality. How could a man conform – as he was required to do as a member of an England corps that placed great store by discipline and camaraderie – when he played the game in such exotically different fashion to everyone else? His method of batting was a bespoke piece of craftsmanship resembling no known design. Every time he whipped the ball through midwicket, every time he executed a reverse sweep or jumped around to face a delivery left-handed, every time he telescoped his arms forward to smother the ball's spin or swerve, he was making a unilateral declaration of independence from the world. The more success he achieved playing this way, the more his self-belief grew, the more convinced he became that he was destined to march to the beat of his own drum.

Two key characteristics set him apart. One was his sheer size.

When people talk about Pietersen and size, many think first of his ego, but without his physical proportion – all 6ft 4in of him – he would not remotely have been the batsman he was. Most of the very greatest batting practitioners were nothing like so tall; many were under 5ft 10in and agile movers around the crease. Big men tend to be slower on their feet and vulnerable to short-pitched bowling, and one of the shortcomings of Pietersen's game during his days at KwaZulu-Natal was a weakness against the bouncer. But what Pietersen's height helped give him was power, and the scope to hit the ball on top of the bounce, but above all it gave him reach – and he used every inch of his reach to his advantage. Reach offered him control of a bigger area of the pitch and he used it the better to defend, and the better to attack. Reach allowed him to routinely get closer to the pitch of the ball than perhaps any major batsman in history. 'I've got long reach and my hands generally help me out when I get myself into trouble,' he explained during his batting master-class for Sky Sports TV in August 2013.

His size was evident in his pre-delivery routine, a process laden with tics, including two little bends of the knees as he prepared to crouch into a stroke, a manoeuvre not required of smaller men. His face would go through a series of grimaces that meant god-knows-what and he would hitch his shirt over his front shoulder in the most irritating fashion. There was further ugliness on the way, too, because his elbows stabbed the air sharply in the course of most shots. Nor was he the smoothest of runners between the wickets. But, oh boy, the shots themselves were usually things of utter majesty, crushing certainty of execution combined with power in a way that left many bowlers feeling utterly helpless.

The other distinctive feature was his extravagant tendency to hit balls through the leg side. During his early days with England, this was seen by many good judges as a likely weakness that might prevent him succeeding in Test match cricket, if not the less technically demanding one-day game (he was also reckoned susceptible to the moving ball outside the off stump, but then who wasn't?). Using his exceptional reach and a strong bottom hand, he whipped balls directed at his stumps or even outside off stump through this region, a strategy carrying high risk: if he missed, he ran a serious danger of falling lbw. But he rarely missed.

It was remarkable to behold and his habit of standing tall on only his front leg as the ball skimmed the turf wide of mid-on earned the shot the nickname of the 'Flamingo', which aptly captured the beauty of the moment. If such a big man could ever look balletic, he did in that instant. One of the reasons Pietersen was not a big cutter of the ball was that he was able to pull balls through his favoured leg side that others would aim square of the wicket on the off side. Being essentially a front-foot player, he could also play square drives off the front foot to balls that others would go back and across to.

'He played some amazing shots for a guy new to international cricket,' Geraint Jones, a team-mate recalled of Pietersen's early games with England. 'A lot of guys get wrapped up in how they think they should play as an international cricketer and forget what got them to that level. Kev never had that problem.

Standing at the other end, watching him take balls from outside off stump and put them through midwicket was a humbling experience. How do you follow that?' Pietersen was unrepentant about his leg-side bias: 'I know where people are coming from, saying "You're wristy, you often use the leg side," but that's where I score all my runs, so why not hit it there?'

The origins of this proclivity probably lay in youthful games of squash, a sport that demands good coordination of eye, hand and wrist, but also in the peculiarities of the games of back-yard cricket he played with his father and brothers, as he explained in an interview in 2006. 'There was a small area about three metres wide between the garage and the house. We chalked a wicket on the wall at the back and bowled at each other from about ten metres . . . We played one hand one bounce, and you were out if you hit the wall on the full. You had to manoeuvre the ball to stay in. We did that for hours every day. My dad said to me recently, "I never believed you'd bring the shots you played in the back yard into the Test arena."'

The key word is 'manoeuvre' because no one ever man-oeuvred the ball better through the leg side. Revealingly, given Pietersen's later penchant for reverse-sweeps and switch-hits, he also said that some days the Pietersens *père et fils* would decree that they could only bat left-handed, just to make things more interesting. However it came about, he had wonderful 'hands'.

Pietersen's on-side game underpinned a broader strategy. With the leg side generally less populated with fielders, it proved an immensely productive area for him. When opposing captains then bolstered their defences on that side of the wicket, Pietersen would switch his attack to the off side, some-times through the use of the reverse-sweep and the switch-hit, a stroke he introduced to international cricket when he played it twice to hit sixes off New Zealand medium-pacer Scott Styris during a one-day international at Durham in 2008 (rather than merely switching his hands on the bat handle, as he did to reverse-sweep, he also turned around in his stance, effectively batting as a left-hander). There was an immediate debate as to whether it was a legal stroke – a bowler had to inform the bats-man which arm he was to bowl with, should not the batsman have to offer a similar courtesy? – but MCC, the guardians of the Laws of Cricket, gave it the green light. Most experts judged it a difficult shot and an exciting innovation. 'It is a sign of genius that a player can make the laws of a game look fool-ish while not obviously cheating,' wrote Michael Atherton in *The Times*.

As Pietersen saw it, there were three scoring areas – the leg side, the off side and straight – and he could open them up in turn. Once Twenty20 cricket became established, batsmen generally became more adept at targeting all 360 degrees of the field, but he was doing this during his time at Nottinghamshire in the early 2000s. 'He thought everybody should be able to drive on the up like he did,' said Stuart MacGill, a former Nottinghamshire team-mate. 'I said, "Kevin, no one else I have played with can drive on the up through midwicket and extra cover." For him it is normal.' This was what made him so dangerous: opponents could not set fields to him and could not stop him scoring.

He was also, of course, armed with immense power – he hit

the ball as hard as anyone – and an ultra-attacking mindset, as he had to be if he was going to attempt the shots he did. This was why his dismissals tended to attract excessive censure. He was trying to dictate the course of events and that required risk. Like Viv Richards and Brian Lara, he was never better than when taking down the best bowlers in the game. He took on Glenn McGrath and Dale Steyn and won. He left Shane Warne and Muttiah Muralitharan at a loss as to their next moves. He reduced India's spinners to dust on their own baked soil.

Not many batsmen were as tall as Pietersen, so few could replicate all that he did, but he did spawn imitators and, in particular, embolden those who followed him into the England team, such as Eoin Morgan and Jos Buttler, to be unafraid about playing unconventionally. After him, anything went. Confounding reports that he was not a good team man, he also influenced a number of colleagues, encouraging someone such as Stuart Broad to modify his stance as a way to counter fast bowling in the Ashes.

He knew how distinctive he was, and relished it. In an introductory message to an online coaching course called 'Keep Calm – and Smash It' which users could access – for a fee – via www.pitchvision.com, Pietersen stated that his guidance would not be drawing on the MCC coaching manual 'because I truly believe I would never have been a success unless I learned to do it my own way . . . I promise you not a word of dogma.'

WHAT IS striking, looking back, is how long it took Pietersen to stop pestering to be treated as an all-rounder and accept he could make a career as a front-line batsman. One of his main gripes with his coaches and captains at school, at KwaZulu-Natal, at Cannock and with Nottinghamshire, was that they would not allow him to bowl his off-spin more (this from a man who once bowled 55.5 overs in an innings against a touring England XI). When he spent a winter with England's academy in 2003-04, he was still talking about working hard on his bowling; and during the summer of 2004, when he was only a few months away from playing his first games for England, he was lauding his bowling as 'another string to my bow'. There were two things wrong with this. One was that his spin bowling was simply not very good and in any case did not suit his mentality (when he eventually made it into the England side, it was virtually ignored: in his first 18 months as an international cricketer he bowled two overs for 22 runs); the other was that he really did not need any more strings to his bow.

That much ought to have been clear for some time. Back in 1999, when he scored an unbeaten half-century for KwaZulu-Natal against Nasser Hussain's England team in 1999, the way he struck the ball was far from commonplace. Shaun Pollock said he had never seen cleaner hitting from someone of such a young age (Pietersen was 19 at the time). When he next came up against England's leading spinner Phil Tufnell, in a County Championship match in 2001, he again dealt with him with ease, unlike most of his team-mates. Pietersen, who scored 165 not out in the first innings and 65 not out in the second, was dispassionate in his summation: 'He [Tufnell] is a great bowler but I had a plan against him. He didn't really bother me at all.

I got the fielders back, I got them where I wanted them and I milked him. If a bad ball came along I hit it for four.' Well, there you go. Simple.

What was also significant about that innings was the 20-year-old Pietersen employing the reverse sweep to hit Tufnell into the stands. Reverse hits were a much rarer currency then than they later became, but they were already becoming part of Pietersen's plan to manipulate the field. Eighteen months later he spent a winter playing for University in Sydney, where he scored heavily as well as prodigiously fast. The season's report from club captain Peter Murray was full of praise for Pietersen's contributions on and off the field but also revealed the extent to which he was exploring his scoring options. 'No batsman was so breathtaking, terrifying and strong ... if you were a third-grade off-spinner in the nets [as Murray was]. Kevin, on a lot of occasions, managed to perfect his reverse slog-sweep – that's right, REVERSE – and hit me and any other poor bloody trundler well into the Teachers College site well away from our No.2 Oval training area. When he first did this I thought: what an impressive but arrogant display of ability.' Pietersen kept a book during his season in Sydney containing notes about opponents and his plans for them. On the inside cover, he scribbled: 'Keep it fucking interesting.'

Despite such persuasive evidence as to just how special a batting prospect he was, Pietersen appeared to think right up to his international debut that presenting himself as an all-rounder gave him his best chance of breaking into the England side. This suggests either that he doubted he was really good enough to make it purely as a batsman, which seems unlikely even if we accept he was not quite as confident as he led the world to believe; more probably, he knew how good he was but feared others might need more convincing.

It seems he was very conscious of just how unorthodoxly he batted and that it was inevitable sceptics would question whether his methods would translate to the Test arena. And he was right: Michael Vaughan, Pietersen's first England coach, felt he did not have a great defence to start with and Duncan Fletcher felt his technique was only suitable for him to bat at No.5 (except for a handful of occasions, Pietersen never batted higher than No.4 in Tests for this reason). Doubting voices could be heard right up to the time of his first Test century. There had previously been doubts he could cut it in county cricket. 'I've been labelled a bit of a slogger,' he told an interviewer in July 2004. This divergence between how Pietersen saw himself and how he was viewed by others was one of the predominant themes of his career. Generally, Pietersen was quicker than others to identify the things he could do well, but slower than them at realising what he was bad at.

His method of batting was far removed from slogging. When he was absolutely on top of his game and destroying bowling attacks in what seemed like a frenzy, he was actually very much in control. There was nothing wild or impetuous about it. It required a great deal of practice and care to manoeuvre the ball as unerringly as he did. Much was made of Pietersen's appetite for practice, and rightly so: practice, and lots of it, was necessary to keep his game functioning properly.

Asked during his master-class programme what he wanted to take away from a net session, he said: 'Rhythm. I just want to keep the rhythm going. Obviously Old Trafford [his previous Test, where he scored a century against Australia] was a pretty good Test match, batting wise. Staying in the same rhythm, also trying to rein myself in and making sure I play in the straight lines I'd played in at Old Trafford. So I go through everything – I'll drive, I'll pull, I won't cut – I don't cut! – I'll play balls through midwicket, I'll face spinners, I'll sweep, I'll reverse-sweep, I'll hit over the top … I make sure I've ticked every single box.' It was a rock-solid routine that he knew worked for him and was based on watching Lance Klusener, a brutal boundary-hitter in the closing overs of one-day matches for South Africa, practising hitting balls against a bowling machine in the KwaZulu-Natal nets. Klusener targetted hitting straight and through the leg side as the most unprotected parts of the field.

Playing in straight lines, as Pietersen put it, was absolutely crucial, especially to those strokes – such as the 'Flamingo' – which onlookers might have thought of as 'across-the-line' shots. 'The key to this shot,' Pietersen added, 'is that everybody thinks that it is a cross-batted shot through the on side, but actually you are playing it with a straight bat. I only play it well when my bat is coming through in straight lines. It must come down straight through the line of off stump and as you make contact you drop your left wrist. There is a danger of losing the shape. I played it against [Vernon] Philander at The Oval in the first Test [of the 2012 series v South Africa]. I did it to [Shaun]

Pollock and [Glenn] McGrath – those bowlers who build a "trench" from not great pace. I get down [the pitch] to it. They start to wonder if I'm coming or not.'

The consequences of not playing straight could be severe. Steve James, the former Glamorgan and England player, wrote an article in 2008 about how Pietersen was having problems that year with his hands escaping wide in his back-lift so that his bat was not coming down straight – losing him 'whip' with his strokes through midwicket.

Another part of his batting mechanism that had to be in order was his head position. 'You do have to get your head to the ball,' he explained. 'I'm a great believer when batting, it's all about head. I've got no interest in feet. The head is absolutely key and vital to my batting. It helps your weight. Your head is the heaviest part of your body. I know I'm batting well when my head is to the ball. If I'm not, my feet are to the ball, my head's back behind my [front] knee. I call it kissing the ball. When I speak to youngsters I say try and kiss the ball. As soon as the heaviest part of your body goes towards the ball, that's when you are going to strike it better because your eyes look after you.'

Even when Pietersen's game was in good working order he could get caught on the crease early on, and trapped lbw. Duncan Fletcher feared that he was vulnerable to the new ball if conditions were helping it to 'do a bit'. Throughout his career, Pietersen was highly dependent on how firm a base was laid by those ahead of him in the order. The runs Marcus Trescothick, Andrew Strauss and Michael Vaughan scored in the 2005 Ashes, and Strauss, Alastair Cook and Jonathan Trott made in Australia in 2010-11, gave Pietersen the platform to take flagging attacks apart. When the top-order batting failed, as it did in Australia in 2006-07 and 2013-14, Pietersen was more exposed to the new ball and much less likely to come off. He was also, by definition, having to retrieve difficult situations and graft more than suited his attacking style.

'He is a trapeze artist, the fellow who does all the tricks, who gets the crowd oohing and aahing but does so with a safety net,' wrote Mike Selvey in the *Guardian* towards the end of the 2013-14 series. 'Pietersen's safety net has been Cook and Strauss and Trott, steadfast players whose presence has allowed him to express himself with free licence ... That is when he is at his compelling best. At the moment, though, he is attempting, through circumstance, to be something he is not, or more precisely, as the senior batsman, everything to everyone.'

Pietersen's 'reach' was also a big factor in his early success in dealing with fast-medium bowlers such as McGrath. Pietersen realised straightaway that the key to playing McGrath was to get to the pitch of the ball. 'People had to get to McGrath's length,' he said. When McGrath was destroying England in helpful conditions at Lord's in 2005, Pietersen – playing his first Test match – could be heard on the stump microphone shouting down the pitch to his partners, 'You've got to get forward, mate. Get forward to everything.' Partly because he was taller, partly because he alone had thought through the strategy, only Pietersen succeeded.

'Pietersen played completely differently from the rest of the team that day,' Strauss recalled in 2013. 'While we were all desperately trying to hang in there, conscious of the potential danger of Glenn McGrath's new-ball spell, he decided to meet fire with fire. A huge stride down the pitch and an outrageous ability to hit a length ball "on the up" prevented even McGrath from containing him ... His willingness and ability to take on the world's best bowlers make him so watchable and so valuable to a team.'

Pietersen's view was that by 2005 McGrath was not bowling as fast as he had been, but also that he himself was not inclined to concern himself with a bowler's reputation (as many of his team-mates seemed to do). 'I never found facing McGrath that hard,' he told Andrew Flintoff. 'I think I got him at a time when he wasn't bowling as fast as he used to ... when he was finishing. Same as Shaun Pollock, he was knocking people's heads off at the start of his career. You tail off towards the end of your career, you don't bowl as fast, but your line and length is immaculate and you live off your reputation. I never worry about people's reputation. You play the ball, you don't play the man. He bowled a good length which I was able to get out [down the pitch] to, occasionally walk at, and I think that tampered with some of the stuff that he did.'

Pietersen might not have worried about the reputation of bowlers, but some of them were beaten before they started, intimidated not only by his reputation but also his size.

Pietersen's reach was also central to how he played spinners. It helped him defend but also helped him score effectively through sweeps, slog-sweeps and reverse-sweeps: as long as he could meet the pitch of the ball, he was unlikely to be beaten by any turn. Just as he had a method to deal with McGrath in 2005, so he did with Warne, based on no more than a couple of encounters in county cricket for Nottinghamshire against Warne's Hampshire. 'He played pretty good [in those games],' Warne said. 'He picked every delivery. He jumped onto the front foot when I bowled a flipper. He knows exactly what's going on.'

Pietersen hit Warne for a number of sixes during the 2005 Tests, most of them from slog-sweeps, some played at what seemed to hyper-anxious England supporters like the most foolhardy moments. 'His play against Shane Warne in 2005 announced him as the team's most ambitious and destructive player of spin in modern times,' said Strauss. So successful was he that in the first innings at Adelaide during the 2006-07 series, Warne was forced to go on the defensive, bowling round the wicket into Pietersen's pads in an effort to stop him scoring. On that occasion, Pietersen accepted the reduced returns in exchange for knowing that Warne wasn't going to get him out.

During the 2006 Sri Lanka series, he worked Muttiah Muralitharan, the world's best off-spinner, so relentlessly to the leg side at Lord's that Murali posted seven men there, then helped himself on the off side. In the following game at Edgbaston, he employed the same tactics, only this time – to widespread astonishment – he reverse-swept Murali high into the stand. The reverse-sweep became a pretty standard ploy for such situations, where a spinner was trying to dry him up by bowling into the rough to a packed leg-side field and with only three men on the off side (slip, backward point, mid-off). Given the gaps on that side of the field, he reckoned it was pretty much a free hit. The switch-hit permitted him to get more power into the shot than he would manage with a reverse-sweep, but was again viewed as a pretty safe option given the field-setting.

The only problem he encountered with the switch-hit was timing the switch correctly: during his match-winning century in Colombo in 2012, he was warned by the umpires for altering his stance before off-spinner Tillekaratne Dilshan's back foot had landed. When Dilshan saw what Pietersen was intending to do, he aborted his run-up, leading to stalemate. Pietersen said he was unaware that he was not permitted to alter his stance before the bowler entered his delivery stride, but MCC had introduced this minor refinement in 2010 after further consideration as to whether Pietersen (and others such as Australia's David Warner who followed his initiative) was gaining an unfair advantage with the switch-hit.

While Pietersen turned his height into an asset in many respects, it did make life tough for him against the short ball. Big men become targets whereas smaller men can more easily weave out of the way. But he was courageous enough to take it on, using his quick eye to hook and pull to devastating effect, as he did against Brett Lee during his famous century at The Oval in 2005. His duel with Lee that day was pivotal in the outcome of the match and the series, and it was one that Pietersen won after plundering 35 off 13 balls from Lee early into the final afternoon session.

It was far from a smooth ride though. Lee peppered him before lunch and he was fortunate to survive. Lee bowled him a first-ball bouncer that clipped his shoulder and was caught at slip, Billy Bowden making an excellent decision to rule it not out. He was dropped by Warne at slip and was nearly caught at gully defending another bouncer. Pietersen asked Vaughan during the lunch break how he thought he should play and Vaughan urged him to play his usual attacking game. Pietersen's opinion though was that although Lee bowled very fast he did not bowl particularly well. 'When you [the batsman] start flashing at balls, the best thing [for the bowler] to do is to hang a ball outside the off stump. If you look at that spell he never bowled me any good balls in any good areas to produce a nick. It was either short or it was at my stumps.'

Not every fast bowler was as generous as Lee that day. Pietersen had problems with the short ball during the winter of the 2006-07 when Mitchell Johnson bounced him out during the Champions Trophy in India and Lee himself gave him a sterner examination during the Ashes in Australia. He also got into difficulties during the 2009-10 tour of South Africa, as he explained during his Sky master-class. 'I struggled ... crouched in my crease. I was going on to the back foot, but like a boxer on the ropes. You have to be on your front foot. I remember when I was growing up Jonty Rhodes saying that it is easier to go back once you are forward than go forward when you are back. Bowlers talk about [bowling] short ball, short ball, [then] nick him off from a length ...

[as a batsman] you have to look out for the full ball because that's the one that can get you out.'

The problems of that South Africa tour didn't last long. A few months later he was pulverising Morne Morkel and Dale Steyn, South Africa's spearheads, in a World Twenty20 match in Barbados. Admittedly this was in a situation in which they weren't as free to pepper him with short balls as they would have been in a Test match, but at Headingley in 2012 he tore them to shreds when they were, and when they ratcheted up the aggression further by attacking him from round the wicket.

Pietersen said that anticipation and instinct were key to dealing with a bowler of Steyn's pace and that one of the shots he played in that innings of 149 – a pull through midwicket – ranked among the two best he had played. Recalling the moment in *All Out Cricket* in January 2014, he said: 'It was one of those shots when the bowler is running up and you're anticipating – and sometimes anticipation leads you down the wrong path – and that ball, having anticipated from the way that Dale ran in and from what I'd done previously and how his mindset was and the state of the game, it was one of those balls that I just knew the shot to play. I just thought, *this* is the only ball that he can bowl and the only ball that he's going to bowl. I had the shot pre-planned in my head and it hit the middle of the bat and it just looked so ... *slow* in the way it just ... *went*.' That performance must rank among his most brilliant, especially given all that was going on behind the scenes between him and the other England players and the

ECB at the time with regard to text messages and his pleas to be given more time at the IPL.

He returned to the value of good instincts in dealing with raw pace after being tested by Mitchell Johnson operating at a rarefied level during the 2013-14 Ashes, tweeting: 'When you [are] facing someone as quick as Mitchell, your instinct occasionally makes you do things you shouldn't. Pace causes indecision!'

It would be wrong, though, to say that Pietersen had a particular problem playing fast bowling or the short ball. He coped with Johnson better than most team-mates and was out to him only twice during the series. Whatever the type of bowling, central to him batting well was regular practice and regular maintenance of his method. For that he needed to be working closely with coaches who understood the intricacies of his game and whom he implicitly trusted.

4

PIETERSEN AND RESPECT

IT WAS often said that Pietersen managed to fall out with every major team he was involved with. The implication was that he was the common denominator in a whole lot of trouble. More specific was the charge that anyone with the power to tell him what to do – whether it was a captain, coach or possibly administrator – presented a challenge to his ego and his self-appointed status as cricketing superstar. This was not quite the case. He certainly did not fall out with all his superiors. There were several people who captained or coached him with whom he got on very well: for example Graham Ford, Clive Rice and Rod Marsh as coaches, and Michael Vaughan as captain. Indeed, it could be argued that one of the difficulties was that he actually got on with them *too* well and as a result tended to look upon alternatives in an unforgiving light. It certainly was not true that he did not respect authority. There were some in positions of authority he revered.

Once he came to a conclusion about someone, he wasn't inclined to change his mind. He played alongside someone, or worked under them, and took a view. After that, what was the point in revising his opinion? He knew his own mind, didn't he? It is a small step from living by the power of self-belief to living by the power of your own opinions, and when he said he backed his own judgement, he meant it in every regard. And the better he became as a player, the more confident and outspoken he was. Altering a judgement smacked of weakness and indecision.

It also happened to be in the nature of things that captains and coaches depended for their survival on the support of their players, players who were familiar with the idea of others constantly passing judgement on them. So, when Ford left Natal in 1998 and Rice left Nottinghamshire in 2002, and were replaced by men Pietersen didn't rate as highly, his views were not hard to fathom. Similarly, when he found himself as England captain working alongside a head coach, Peter Moores, whom he thought was not up to the job, he did not hesitate to speak up, or to suggest Ford as the man to replace him.

Pietersen was most enthusiastic about those who showed a steadfast belief in what he could do, who were able to help refine his game and offer constant encouragement. Those that gave him such attention, he liked and championed; from those that didn't, he withdrew his respect. Considering there were ten other players in a team, and perhaps 15 other players in a tour squad, this probably categorised him as high maintenance, but the potential returns were rich. And, frankly, if a coach or captain was not there to help, what was the point of him? Pietersen's own game was very important to him and he wanted all the help he could get. 'Narcissist or genius? Or both?' Andrew Strauss asked at the opening to an article in the *Sunday Times* about Pietersen on the eve of the 2013 Ashes series. They were reasonable questions.

Ford was the first high-quality coach Pietersen worked with. Ford got him involved in KwaZulu-Natal's age-group teams and helped get him his early games in first-class cricket with KwaZulu-Natal's B team. He was a family friend of the Pietersens and was closely involved in his decision to move to England. He was also one of the first people to predict that Pietersen would play Test cricket. Although they never worked together again on a sustained basis until Ford joined Surrey as coach in 2014, the two remained in contact and Pietersen continued to regard Ford as a key adviser. When Pietersen developed a technical problem in 2010, it was Ford rather than Andy Flower's team of England coaches who identified the fault, during a short stint Pietersen spent with KwaZulu-Natal in the build-up to the Ashes tour of Australia. According to Pietersen, within three or four shots of his first net Ford noticed there was something wrong with his hip position and head movement, and once that was rectified his game returned to full working order. 'He understands my game,' Pietersen said at Surrey's press day in March 2014. 'I love hitting with Fordy. He is my mentor. He gets me.'

Rice, another South African, and in his day a formidable all-rounder who was denied the chance to play Test cricket by the anti-apartheid sport boycott, was an even more important figure in his development. He saw Pietersen play as a 17-year-old at a Nuffield Cricket Week, which were useful windows onto emerging talent in South Africa, and after subsequently hearing, while director of cricket at Nottinghamshire, that Pietersen was scoring heavily for league side Cannock offered him a three-year county contract on scant evidence. Rice immediately got to grips with Pietersen's technique, altering his foot movements to make him less vulnerable to the moving ball in English conditions; Pietersen had been inclined to plant his front foot and play around his front pad.

Rice ran Nottinghamshire in autocratic style but recognised Pietersen as a special talent, treating him in a paternalistic, sympathetic manner. Although he considered him as a *bona fide* batsman, he started him off at No.6 to give him time to settle before moving him up the order, and setting him tough but attainable targets. Rice's view was that coaches and managers who weren't strong tended to find it difficult to deal with brash players like Pietersen; his own approach was to cut Pietersen some slack, because he felt he was good enough to deliver on the field, and give him as much attention as he needed.

This grated with some Notts players but they got short shrift from Rice, who demanded that they work around the team's best match-winner. Pietersen himself hung on Rice's every word, eagerly absorbing all the advice on offer. 'Kevin didn't come to England to play for Notts or for England, he came to play for Clive Rice,' said Mick Newell, assistant coach to Rice before taking over from him in 2002. 'There was a huge respect from him towards Clive and he definitely wanted Clive to be impressed with what he did ... Kevin took anything Clive said on board. If Clive had said "bat left-handed" he would have done.' No wonder Rice said, 'He listens well.' No wonder Pietersen was devastated when Rice was sacked after a run of bad results. 'I bitterly disagreed with Notts's decision,' Pietersen recalled. 'I had lost my father figure, the man who had brought me to England and Notts, the man I believed in one hundred percent. His methods were my methods.'

Newell said that he was not sure Pietersen much cared whether Notts won or lost once Rice had gone, although he continued to train hard and make sure his own performances were good. As with Ford, Pietersen stayed in regular touch with Rice, who continued to advise him right through to his time as England captain, and beyond.

Pietersen's involvement with Rod Marsh was only brief but it came during another crucial phase in his career. Marsh, a former Australia wicketkeeper-batsman and a hardliner like Rice, had recently been appointed director of the ECB's new national academy at Loughborough University as well as an England selector. Pietersen was a member of the 2003-04 academy in-take and with England selection in sight he was more focused than ever on stating his case. The academicians were put through a tough training regime at Loughborough before undertaking an even more arduous tour of India, where Pietersen's success with the bat was in stark contrast to the fortunes of the team.

Marsh may have been a hard taskmaster but he also knew how to manage people and earned Pietersen's gratitude for allowing him to commute from his home in Nottingham rather than make him stay on campus. 'Me and Marshy gelled really nicely,' he said. 'I respect him as much as anyone, the way he treats people as human beings.'

Marsh also taught him a big lesson about playing spin. Pietersen was alarmed after falling twice to leg-spin early on during the tour of India. Marsh told him to watch team-mate Graham Napier play spin in the nets. Pietersen duly stood alongside and watched, and after a few minutes went over to Marsh and said, 'I understand what to do now.' Marsh was impressed with how quickly Pietersen solved the problem: 'It was freakish. It was just footwork. You have to move all the way forward or all the way back … Kevin learned that in ten minutes. That's highly unusual.'

For the rest of the tour, Pietersen was untroubled by the many spinners he came up against and reeled off four hundreds as well as a score of 94. Marsh rated Pietersen the second most talented batsman after Ricky Ponting that he worked with in 15 years as head of academies in Australia and England. 'I had my fears whether he would take to the academy,' Marsh added. 'He had the reputation in some circles as being arrogant, not listening and maybe doing things his own way. But every one of us here would give him a glowing report … He is a fine cricketer and a fine bloke.'

Marsh, too, was instrumental in encouraging Pietersen to bury his differences with Nottinghamshire and return to play for them in 2004, telling him in essence that the only thing that could spoil his chances of playing for England once his qualification period was complete was an ugly fall-out with his county. 'Get your head down and play for Notts,' was the message. And Pietersen did just that. Marsh's sensible words, and the carrot of international cricket, brought him into line.

Pietersen's relationships with his first England coach and captain, Duncan Fletcher and Michael Vaughan, were excellent. Fletcher spotted Pietersen's potential within his first two games for England in Zimbabwe in 2004 and resolved to keep him on for the one-day series in South Africa from which Pietersen was originally omitted. Fletcher was impressed by how deeply Pietersen thought about his cricket and when Fletcher resigned at the 2007 World Cup Pietersen, along with Strauss, wrote him letters expressing 'their whole-hearted praise and thanks'.

Like Rice, Fletcher for much of his time in charge thought it best to bat Pietersen down the order because he felt he could be exposed by new-ball movement. 'I've got great respect for Duncan Fletcher,' Pietersen said in 2008. 'He is one of the best batting coaches I ever worked with . . . He treated me brilliantly and I loved playing for him.'

Their one spat came after Pietersen returned home early from a tour of Pakistan in late 2005 with a rib injury. Fletcher had warned him to keep a low profile, yet Pietersen almost immediately wrote in his *News of the World* column in support of Darren Gough's recall to the ODI side, then popped up in the TV audience when Gough appeared on *Strictly Come Dancing*. Fletcher felt Pietersen's support for Gough implicitly undermined those who were actually in the team and phoned him up, incensed: 'Who do you think you are? You've only been on the scene two minutes!' Fletcher was later gratified to note that Pietersen subsequently expressed regret for mistakes such as this that he made in the period following the 2005 Ashes win.

Speaking in 2013, Vaughan, while acknowledging that he was fortunate to have had the best of Pietersen between 2004 and 2008, described him as professional, driven and a real pleasure to work with. It was evident that Vaughan's man-management skills came to the fore in his handling of Pietersen and Andrew Flintoff, who also had the potential to be difficult. In Vaughan's judgement, Flintoff was the hardest player he had to deal with; he could be a 'genius' on the field but was inclined to be lazy off it – unlike Pietersen.

Recognising that the best England sides had blockbuster players such as Ian Botham, Flintoff and Pietersen, Vaughan resolved to find a way to get the best out of his two biggest stars. 'To me, part of managing them was exercising a bit of live-and-let-live,' he wrote in his autobiography in 2009. 'To a degree, you have to accept the whole package.' If either got out to a risky shot, he wasn't inclined to criticise them and positively encouraged Pietersen to play freely. Of the period when England were first considering selecting Pietersen for the Test side in 2005, Vaughan added: 'It certainly did not bother me that he was a Flash Harry off the pitch at that stage, our very own king of bling. What I did not want was a team of clones and I thought that, with the spine of the team that we had, we could live with this sort of maverick. The question I was wondering about most was how he and Flintoff were going to be together, and that was to prove an ongoing issue. It is bound to be when you have two players who love the limelight and being at the centre of the action.' Vaughan's first impressions of Pietersen, in fact, were that 'he was a real nice kid ... gentle'.

Vaughan accepted that the most naturally talented players found it hard to sit through the technical talk of team meetings. 'I tried to limit that side for the likes of [Flintoff] and KP and allow them just to play and express themselves. We never wanted the team meetings to go on too long for that reason.' Subsequent England managements weren't inclined to be so charitable when Pietersen, by his own admission, struggled to listen closely. Vaughan also recommended Pietersen to captain England across all formats when he himself resigned as Test captain in 2008.

Pietersen, in turn, recognised his debt to Vaughan. He was instrumental in Vaughan being awarded a central contract a few weeks after Vaughan's resignation as Test captain and he lobbied for his recall to the team the following winter when he himself was captain. In fact, Vaughan never played for England again but that was down to other selectors, not Pietersen. Around the same time, with Pietersen's problems with Peter Moores coming to the surface, Vaughan was briefly used as go-between when Pietersen was reluctant to talk directly to the ECB. All of which may help explain why Vaughan was so publicly critical of the decision to sack Pietersen in 2014.

Pietersen also struck up warm relationships with his coaches in the Indian Premier League. Trent Woodhill, who was an assistant coach at Delhi Daredevils when Pietersen played for the franchise in 2012, said of Pietersen at the time his relationship with England was starting to hit trouble in Australia in 2013-14: 'England do not know what a jewel they have. Kevin is the best team man I've been involved with.' When Pietersen was unveiled as Delhi captain in April 2014, he immediately struck up a rapport with Gary Kirsten, the former South African opener turned coach. 'Gary and I sing off a similar hymn-sheet ... He's got the personality that makes you want to really be successful for him and the franchise. He makes you feel happy about yourself. Everything that comes out of his mouth makes sense.'

These words might have been customary platitudes trotted out before a ball had been bowled in anger, but when it came to coaches in particular, first impressions were often vital for Pietersen.

ABSORBED IN the potentialities of his own game, Pietersen may not have always seen cricket as a team game. There simply wasn't the time, what with trying to be recognised by Natal and then striving to be worth a place in the Nottinghamshire side. If he couldn't convince his county of his Englishness, he could at least put his status as the best batsman in the team beyond argument. He was so busy training and practising and *thinking* about how to get the best out of himself, he might have been forgiven for regarding team as a secondary consideration. In any case, wasn't that what every player was supposed to do? Sort out yourself and the whole would look after itself.

For Pietersen, occasional conflicts arose between what might best suit him and what might best suit the team. What was the right course if a particular coach – Clive Rice, for example – was good for him but not good for the team? What happened if he was scoring lots of runs but the team was still losing? Perhaps the others should try harder? Maybe they couldn't. Perhaps they could play like him? Certainly they could not. When Geoff Boycott found himself the best batsman in the Yorkshire side by a country mile, he took consolation in being the biggest fish in a small pond. Pietersen contemplated upgrading the pond.

Pietersen was clear in his own mind that getting rid of Rice in the summer of 2002 was a mistake and his dissatisfaction immediately grew when one of the first acts of Mick Newell, Rice's successor, was to drop him from the side. Admittedly Pietersen had been going through a lean patch, but he felt Newell was putting him on some sort of trial (which he proba- bly was). If that was the intention, it worked. After a short break, Pietersen returned to the first team to play better than ever and record a career-best 254 against Middlesex as a late run saw Notts gained promotion to the Championship first divi- sion. However, fault-lines in Pietersen's relationships with Newell and Jason Gallian, the captain, opened up during a tough season in 2003 when Notts were relegated after winning only their first and last Championship games. With Pietersen's own form good, he grew increasingly frustrated and increasingly vocal. Gallian described the once-quiet outsider as 'raucous and opinionated . . . and very controversial'.

Things came to a head during a home Championship match against Kent in late August. After Notts had been dismissed for just 177, with Pietersen scoring exactly 100 off 99 balls (including two sixes and a four off Muttiah Muralitharan, who was withdrawn from the attack after just one over), he marched off the field and told Newell that he would not be fielding because (according to Newell) 'this lot are shit'. One of the senior players, New Zealand all-rounder Chris Cairns, who was captain that day, immediately intervened. Newell recounted: 'He [Cairns] got up and just took Kevin into my little office and held him up against the wall by the throat and gave him a bit of a verbal tongue-lashing in regards to his commitment to the rest of the team. It was just words, no punches were thrown. There wasn't a huge amount said from KP.'

Pietersen fielded after all but, again according to Newell, emotionally detached himself from the team for much of the rest of the season. He played two terrible innings against Essex before announcing during the following game with Middlesex that he would be leaving the club. That he still had one year left on his contract did not seem to register. When Pietersen later heard that Gallian – frustrated and angry at the prospect of losing his best player – had smashed up Pietersen's bat and tossed it over the Trent Bridge balcony after end-of-season drinks which Pietersen did not bother to attend, he confronted his captain on the phone and refused to accept his apologies. There was no ameliorating him: when Gallian tried to speak to him a few weeks later, a message came back via the club that he should not try to contact Pietersen again as he had taken out a restraining order on him. With Pietersen seeking release from the last year of his contract, and Notts refusing to cooperate, a date was set for an industrial tribunal and only Rod Marsh's late intervention persuaded Pietersen to back down and see out his contract.

'I don't really like discussing that incident [smashing Pietersen's bat],' Gallian recalled in a BBC Radio profile of Pietersen broadcast in September 2012. 'All I'd like to say about that season was that Kevin had done things and I'd done things probably we both regret. Things I don't really want to go into too much detail [about] ... Working with him, the dynamics of it, for Kevin it has to be respect.'

Once he had made the decision to stay, Pietersen's behaviour altered dramatically. It was as though nothing had ever been wrong. There was no further trouble, although it undoubtedly helped that Nottinghamshire played much better to win the Championship second division and the Australian David Hussey gave him some competition for the title of the best batsman in the side. There was even talk towards the end of the season of him signing a new contract, but Pietersen's agent demanded more money than the county was prepared to offer. The year after he left, Nottinghamshire won the title.

Surprisingly, these incidents did not appear to persuade Pietersen as to the advisability of diplomacy. Simon Jones, a good friend of Pietersen's, recounted how during their winter together at the ECB academy during 2003-04 – in other words at the very time when feelings over Pietersen's breakdown with Newell and Gallian were at their most raw – Pietersen got into an argument with a team-mate he did not rate and told him: 'I've got more talent in my little finger than you have in your entire body.'

There were echoes too of the Nottinghamshire situation of 2003 when England went through their first serious run of defeats since Pietersen had joined them during the Ashes tour of 2006-07. Pietersen did well, scoring 490 runs in the five Tests, but England were whitewashed 5-0. There were no flash-points as such but he again withdrew himself from the team, to the disappointment of Andrew Flintoff, the captain.

Pietersen admitted in his radio interview with Flintoff that it was only after his struggle with left-arm spin in 2010 that he understood 'bad stuff'. He said: 'Until you understand what the bad stuff is, you [can't] relate to situations and I don't think I related to that situation [in 2006-07]. I thought, "I got five hundred runs … why the hell did we lose, why do we keep getting smashed?" I think that might have rubbed off the wrong way on some people.' Flintoff said during the same programme: 'There were tricky times … he knows exactly how many runs he got and what he did; however, he could have given a little bit back in the dressing-room, helping people out who (1) weren't as good as him and (2) were not having a great trip. It's not just about scoring runs.'

Moores, who took over as coach from Fletcher in 2007, was never a comfortable fit with Pietersen. He was too confrontational with several senior players, including Vaughan the captain (though not, significantly, Flintoff). Asked later what the problem was between himself and Pietersen, Moores replied: 'The whole issue revolved around respect. It was about whether he felt he respected my view and whether together we could have moved it [the England team] forward.'

Pietersen's relationship with Andy Flower and Andrew Strauss – who succeeded Moores and himself in 2009 – was more complex. In many ways, Flower was similar to Moores, under whom he cut his teeth in the England set-up, and when Pietersen proposed the removal of Moores he wanted Flower, his assistant, gone too. But Pietersen would have held Flower's achievements as a player – he was a former No.1 Test-ranked batsman with Zimbabwe – in higher regard than he did those of Moores, who never came close to playing for England.

'Reputations don't come into it with Andy Flower if he believes someone needs knocking into line,' Graeme Swann said in his 2011 autobiography. 'He is not afraid to tell us a few home truths, irrespective of the player or their record. He will just say: "That is not acceptable, that doesn't work in this team."'

In one of his first team meetings, Flower challenged his players to be more honest about themselves. Pietersen was confronted strongly, as Mark Garaway, the team analyst, recounted in Steve James's forensic study of the modern England team, *The Plan*: 'I remember one conversation where they were challenging KP and somebody challenged him about his lifestyle, about being in the papers all the time and living in Chelsea. KP quite rightly went at them, saying, "I train as hard, if not harder, than anybody else, and I believe my results speak for themselves. I can back it up."' Some senior players came to Pietersen's defence, including Flintoff and Harmison, who hadn't always seen eye-to-eye with him.

But Pietersen could speak glowingly of the Flower–Strauss partnership and he had few issues with Strauss until 2012, when Pietersen's desire to have more time off to play in the IPL became a source of friction. The revelation of Pietersen's texts to the South Africa opposition shocked Strauss in part because he believed he and Pietersen got on well, while Pietersen himself expressed regret at what happened that summer. 'Andrew Strauss is a great friend,' he recalled shortly after his sacking by England. 'I was just in a bad space. We were not having a great relationship at that time.'

Flower and Strauss found Pietersen's maverick streak much harder to accommodate than Vaughan. 'Players who are more than happy to tear up the cricketing rule-book do not enjoy being contained by rules off the field,' Strauss wrote in 2013. 'Within the team environment he [Pietersen] was never comfortable when being forced to toe the team line. Dressed up in a suit like everyone else at team functions and standing on ceremony was far too constraining for such a free spirit. Any opportunity to display his individuality, from wearing distinctive shoes to driving a different car, was jumped at eagerly. The inevitable planning meetings, deciding on tactics and the like, tended to bore him ... His instinctive nature put him at odds with the type of meticulous planning that myself and Andy Flower tended to favour. This attitude at times caused friction. The prevailing culture of always putting the team first was tested.'

OLD-SCHOOL cricketers might have shaken their heads at the thought of a 23-year-old taking out a restraining order against his county captain or trying to extricate himself from his contract via an industrial tribunal, but this was the way the modern game was going. Player power was on the rise. Thanks to the liberalisation of employment laws, professional cricketers were freer than ever to move in search of employment, and a new format of the game – Twenty20 – introduced into the English county game in 2003 was soon to transform the relationship between players and their traditional employers.

Whereas once they might hope to earn serious money only as internationals, and therefore had to abide by the wishes of their masters, the Twenty20 craze opened up an alternative line of work through cash-rich franchises. The first World Twenty20 was staged late in 2007 and, crucially, was won by India, whose arm had needed twisting to take part. With their new-found enthusiasm for 20-over cricket came their financial muscle. A few weeks later, an Indian Cricket League was launched with former West Indies legend Brian Lara enticed out of retirement by the prospect of a $1 million contract. Early in 2008 what would prove the definitive model emerged in the shape of the Indian Premier League. When its first season opened, nearly 50 players owned contracts worth $400,000-plus if they played the duration. At a stroke, the balance of power tipped towards the players, who now began to

see themselves as individual businesses, not 24/7 serfs inden-
tured to all-powerful boards.

Twenty20 cricket seemed a perfect fit for Pietersen as it positively encouraged innovation and audacity. In the early days of
the county competition, he – like most people – regarded 20-
over cricket as a bit of a laugh. 'It's just a good slog,' he said in
2004. 'It's only two hours of cricket so we enjoy it and just have
some fun. It's a flip of a coin sometimes to decide who's going
to win.' But once the coins started flowing into the players'
pockets, attitudes shifted. The rewards were simply too large to
ignore. When Chris Gayle, the West Indies batsman, texted
Pietersen a whole series of dollar signs to convey what the IPL
was going to be like, he was already preaching to a converted
man. 'Twenty20 will be the new form of one-day cricket for
sure,' Pietersen said in June 2008. 'In the next couple of years
fifty-over cricket is going to be something of the past. To me,
Test cricket is still the best. There is no better feeling than getting a Test match hundred. But Twenty20 is a game that is at
the forefront of our thought patterns.'

Naturally, national boards were nervous. They could veto any
player appearing in the IPL, but that was a dangerous route to go
down. England and West Indies, whose seasons directly clashed
with the tournament, quickly arranged a series of rival events
funded by Allen Stanford, a Texan businessman, the first of them
an eye-opening contest for $1 million per man scheduled for
November 2009, but this was like attempting to race the multi-
national IPL juggernaut in a three-wheeler. Every country had to
make compromises to accommodate their players' enthusiasm

for the IPL. Pakistan and Sri Lanka simply cleared their schedules by scrapping a Test series, and when MS Dhoni, the India captain, played the first season of IPL and then announced he was missing a Test series because he was tired, no one dared try to stop him.

The ECB took a hard line in the IPL's first year, when no England players took part, and it initially promised to be equally tough in 2009 when it was concerned about how preparations might be affected for a home Ashes series. 'Kevin Pietersen receives not insignificant rewards,' said Giles Clarke, the ECB chairman. 'We are putting on board significant rewards for winning series. People who turn up exhausted from the IPL are not necessarily going to be in a position to help their fellows earn those rewards. Cricket is a team game.'

Much to England's relief, Pietersen initially reaffirmed his commitment to England. 'There's no way in this world I'll turn my back on England,' he said. 'I love playing for England and there'll be nothing that will lure me away from England just yet. It's a great challenge, challenging myself against the best players in the world both in Test cricket and one-day international cricket. Yes I know there is interest [from the IPL] and yes there have been offers, but it's not something I'm particularly interested in.' Those with sharp ears, though, did not miss the words, 'just yet'.

Inevitably, the ECB softened its position for the IPL's second year, although to almost a derisory extent. England players were granted just a 15-day window in the calendar to take part and a few entered the auction in February 2009. Neither Pietersen nor Flintoff was to be disappointed, attracting the biggest full-season valuations for any overseas players of $1.55 million, Pietersen with Royal Challengers Bangalore and Flintoff with Chennai Super Kings. The size of their deals only emphasised the riches available to those unencumbered by other commitments during the IPL season.

It was something that would give Pietersen considerable food for thought, especially as he had by then been through the most traumatic episode of his career.

5

PIETERSEN AND CAPTAINCY

PIETERSEN was an odd choice as England captain. He had no history of leading teams, not at school, not in age-group cricket, not at county level. He'd once been put in charge of Nottinghamshire second XI for a one-day game and scored a match-winning century, but was still never asked back. Five weeks before his official appointment, he had stood in for one match as one-day captain in the absence of the suspended Paul Collingwood.

As a rank-and-file player, he found it hard to conform and if there was one thing a captain wanted from his players it was conformity. But the biggest problem was that he was prone to mistakes: as a batsman he took the sort of risks that could look foolish when they failed to come off – in the very last Test match before his appointment there was what Michael Vaughan described as 'a little bit of a kerfuffle in the dressing-room' after Pietersen, in a game England were trying to save, holed out trying to clear long on for the six that would have brought up his hundred.

Furthermore, he also had an unfortunate habit of saying more than was necessary, talking himself up or blurting out a criticism of someone else. Graeme Swann said of Andrew Strauss: 'He is one of those guys who demand respect ... He always says the right things, whether it be in team meetings or press conferences, and his word is never questioned.' The same could not quite be said of Pietersen. During his first Test in charge, I was one of three newspaper reporters interviewed about England's new leader by Jonathan Agnew on BBC Radio's *Test Match Special* and I said that I thought Pietersen's main challenge would not come from anything on the pitch but whether he could avoid getting into hot water with something he said off it. And so it proved, and much more quickly than anyone could have imagined.

That said, Pietersen did not ask to be made captain. He was chosen by men who should have known better and might have thought twice had they stopped to consider how often English cricket puts the wrong man in charge. But Vaughan's sudden resignation left no time for reflection: the next match was due to start five days later. Vaughan himself recommended, and the selectors wanted, one man to reunite the leadership of the Test and one-day teams (which had been split between Vaughan and Collingwood), and a leader the Australians would respect and fear going into the 2009 Ashes. Pietersen was almost the only credible candidate, several senior players having recently departed. Even so, according to Steve James's study of the modern England team, Giles Clarke, the ECB chairman, was sufficiently concerned at the prospect of a Pietersen captaincy that he considered using his power of veto. He was not the only one to have doubts. Former England captain Michael Atherton wrote in *The Times*: 'I have a horrible feeling that this is going to end in tears.'

Even so, it was Pietersen's fault that he lost the job in the way that he did. Even if Peter Moores himself did not grasp the extent of the new captain's reservations about him, Pietersen ought to have known that his relationship with the coach was likely to be a problem that would need sorting at some stage and that he would need to tread carefully if it was to be resolved in his favour. Vaughan warned him of as much. When Pietersen rang and told him he had been offered the job, Vaughan advised him to take it but to be sure he knew where the boundaries lay on management issues and who had the final say on preparing the team. Along with other senior players, Vaughan and Pietersen had had their problems with Moores's desire to challenge and dictate on a daily basis. But when it came to it, both Pietersen and Moores seemed to think they were in charge. A person with a politician's instinct would have plotted a course of action and bided his time; Vaughan reckoned the captaincy was a job that needed six to nine months of bedding in. But, as ever, Pietersen was a man in a hurry.

That said, he was unlucky. He was dealt some tough hands. His first assignment overseas was the Stanford match in

Antigua for $1 million a man. It was a game that caused acute difficulties within the England camp, with the ECB trying to dress it up as not just being about the money but as something that would also benefit grass-roots cricket in the Caribbean. At one point Pietersen had to sit down with four or five of his players and tell them not to talk to the press in the way that they were because it was conveying the wrong image. Then, 24 hours before the game, Andrew Flintoff proposed that if they won the game the 11 players who took the field should pass on ten percent of their money to the four other squad members, who were supposed to share $1 million between them. This only heightened the unease many already felt, with not everyone comfortable at the thought of giving up $100,000 (Flintoff and Pietersen could afford it more easily than others). In the event, England lost the game heavily and went away empty-handed.

Then, within three weeks of arriving in India, Pietersen's first major tour as captain was thrown into disarray by terrorist attacks on various key sites in Mumbai including the Taj Mahal Hotel where the team would be based. The players left for home before returning en masse two weeks later to complete an amended itinerary that included two Tests in Chennai and Mohali. Pietersen was reckoned to have led his team well during this difficult period, saying the right things, sounding in control and phoning round the players to see if they were happy about returning, although cynics – never in short supply when it came to Pietersen – speculated that he was keen to return to India because of his impending involvement with

Royal Challengers Bangalore in the IPL. It was a period that took its toll and prompted a revealing remark from England's new captain: 'The four-year tenure that captains mostly do is now down to four months.'

On the field he looked less assured. He had done well in his first Test in charge against South Africa at The Oval, scoring a century and leading England to a resounding victory. He encouraged his bowlers with constant chivvying and bum-pats. However, in harsher conditions in India he was much less at ease as all five one-day internationals were lost and India took the Test series 1-0 after stunningly chasing down 387 in Chennai. Graeme Swann, who admittedly had reason not to feel enamoured with Pietersen's leadership because he was often left out of the ODI side in favour of Samit Patel, though he then made his Test debut under him in Chennai, said that Pietersen did not always make him feel at ease. 'I need someone who can calm me down, but Kev could get quite wound up,' he said. 'At one point in India his leadership was reduced to a period of screaming "Fucking bowl fucking straight" at everyone.' But England came up against some brilliant batting from Virender Sehwag and Sachin Tendulkar, and Pietersen was not the first captain to come unstuck in India. Few long-term conclusions could be drawn from what happened on the field.

By his own admission, Pietersen mishandled a decision to drop Harmison from the second Test in Mohali. He conveyed the news the day before the game and Harmison's response was to immediately summon a taxi and return to the hotel. Pietersen recalled: 'Harmy went AWOL for a couple of days . . .

I didn't know how to react. I didn't realise, I didn't know why. Maybe I just did it in the wrong way because I didn't understand where he was coming from. I hadn't been through that [myself].'

When he was unveiled as captain of Delhi Daredevils in 2014, his first captaincy assignment since the England job, Pietersen reflected: 'My mindset has changed a hell of a lot [since then]. When I was thrust into the England captaincy, it was very difficult at that stage as I hadn't been through a load of processes and I've had a load of ups and downs since then. Only when you reach good heights and reasonably low lows do you understand everybody and everything. When you have a family you understand families, when you have kids you understand kids. When I took over the England captaincy I hadn't experienced a lot of those things. For me, understanding people, managing people and getting to grips with how everybody's feeling . . . is vitally important in making sure we are all happy and everyone's fighting for one result.'

The fact Harmison was not reprimanded for his behaviour became a bone of contention with some players during the Mohali Test and contributed to general grumblings about how well the team management was functioning. As when things went wrong between Pietersen and the management in Australia in 2013-14, there were few clues as to the rift that had opened up. It was never a raging feud between Pietersen and Moores, and in fact when Moores was reappointed England coach in April 2014 he said, 'I never fell out with Kevin, Kevin fell out with me . . . I don't have any blame at all.'

Steve James believed that the situation was not helped by Flintoff: 'He and Pietersen never got on in the team environment, a clashing of egos as they jostled for the position of Top Cat. And Flintoff was more than happy to position himself in Moores's camp. He liked the coach from the start, especially when Moores offered to go with him to a specialist's appointment when injured. It was a level of care he never felt he'd received from [Duncan] Fletcher. But was Moores just being cute? Flintoff was a powerful dressing-room presence. I've heard that Moores used that relationship in his defence.'

Pietersen in fact took the decisive step – a step that would lead to the swift departure of himself and Moores and take his own career on a very different path from the one it might otherwise have followed – at an early stage by going to Giles Clarke the day before the first Test in Chennai to voice his concerns about the coach. Pietersen was absolutely right to speak up. If he did not feel he could work with the head coach then he had a duty to say so and his history of taking difficult, unpopular decisions that ultimately worked out for him would have probably convinced him that, however awkward, it was the correct course. However, he may have chosen the wrong man. According to James, had Pietersen gone to his line manager, Hugh Morris, the managing director of England cricket, rather than the board chairman, it might have been possible to resolve things in less drastic fashion. Morris was naturally a conciliator. Even as it was, Pietersen was asked to outline in an email his vision for the future of the team, while attempts were made to keep both men. 'We were seeking to solve the situation managerially,' one board source said. 'The issue was, could they get on, could their heads be banged together?'

The problem was that Pietersen was so strident in his position. He argued that the whole team thought Moores was no good and wanted him to go; when Morris spoke to the players, he found this was not quite the case (although Strauss has subsequently written that many senior players held reservations). He argued that not only Moores had to go but also all of his backroom staff including assistant coach Andy Flower, who was eventually appointed as the new coach. He also threatened to resign if Moores stayed in post, leaving himself little wriggle room in negotiations. Some felt he was not being as clear as he could have been, Vaughan saying: 'I suggested to KP that he really had to explain himself to both his employers and the public and make sure that he got his point across.' Nor did he help himself by sticking to his holiday plans after the India tour was over; on safari in South Africa, he was not as accessible as he might have been.

Pietersen had still not returned from holiday when he was informed via a phone call from Morris that his captaincy was at an end after just five months. It was not a straightforward situation though. The board accepted that Moores had to go too: the dressing-room might not have been as firmly against him as Pietersen suggested, but there were serious question marks over his confrontational style, and if Pietersen was to remain as a player it was hard to see how Moores could continue to command the dressing-room. The problem for Pietersen was that the board felt he couldn't be seen dictating who could be coach.

'He did a great job to start with,' one board member said. 'He could have been very good, if only he had listened and matured.'

PIETERSEN may have messed up, but that was not how he saw it. He believed he was doing what was in the long-term interests of the England team and that it was his duty to speak up. He was stunned to be told by Hugh Morris that his resignation had been accepted; he claimed he never tendered it, merely indicated that he could not continue working with Moores. It took him 20 hours to publicly confirm his 'resignation' and he remained defiant in a radio interview after Andrew Strauss had been named his successor. 'It's been really hurtful what's happened,' he said. 'I know that what I did was definitely not wrong and I did things the right way, the way I was asked to do them by my employers ... I was asked to do something in a strategic manner and by the book and I did everything that I was asked to.' At another point he said he was standing down even though he had 'much more to offer as captain'.

Now where did he stand? Rightly or wrongly, the outsider who had craved – and been granted – acceptance from English cricket's Establishment now felt betrayed by it. Until this point, his relationship with the England team and the ECB had been pretty smooth and he had restated his commitment to the cause whenever he was asked. Media reports that the dressing-room turned against him in his attempts to get Moores removed were not convincingly backed up, although Flintoff confirmed that he had told Pietersen he could not support him. The focus of Pietersen's ire was directed at the board. According to Steve James, he felt betrayed by three officials – unnamed but presumed to be Morris, Clarke and David Collier, the chief executive – who had, he said, assured him that Moores would be removed. He also suspected a plot when reports of a rift between himself and Moores eventually reached the news-papers; he publicly insisted that he had not released any unauthorised information. 'Something was leaked, I don't know who by; I would love to find that person,' he said. James thinks Pietersen thought it was Clarke and that was why Pietersen did not speak to the board chairman for almost a year.

Things would never be quite the same again. Trust, or the lack of it, was something that was often used against Pietersen in the later stages of his England career, but at this earlier stage it became very much an issue for him.

The ECB was conscious enough of Pietersen's hurt to be nervous that he might simply turn his back on England alto-gether; it had, after all, granted him permission to enter the second IPL auction that was less than six weeks away. A team meeting was called in Loughborough. 'Its sole purpose, as far as I could tell, was to make sure that Kev would toe the party line and go along as one of the rank and file,' Graeme Swann recalled in his autobiography. In fact, Pietersen had already made his position clear within days of losing the captaincy in a column in the *News of the World*; he reiterated his commitment '100 percent' to winning games of cricket for England and said he hoped to play for England for another seven years. There was soon further reason for the board's blood pressure to rise with the collapse of the Allen Stanford project, the United States authorities announcing they were investigating him for fraud. It looked like the IPL was set to remain a thorn in the ECB's side.

Pietersen stayed and however hard he tried he could not stop the old insecurities resurfacing. Both his form with the bat and his behaviour were to become more erratic from here on. Up to this point he had played in 45 Tests and scored 4,039 runs at an average of 50.48 with 15 hundreds; subsequently, he would play another 59 Tests for 4,142 runs at an average of 44.53 with only eight hundreds. Normally a player of his quality would have been expected to perform much better after the age of 28, not worse. Obviously, this rather unexpected decline could not be put down purely to the loss of the captaincy. Other factors were at play – he had Achilles and knee injuries to contend with for much of the rest of his England career – but it was no coincidence that he became a less reliable run-scorer once he felt a less secure member of the team. What is also striking is that for much of this second phase of his career, he was playing in an England team that was flourishing under the new captain-coach combination of Strauss and Andy Flower.

Pietersen must have looked on ruefully as he saw Strauss working so productively with a coach he saw eye-to-eye with, even if Pietersen himself held no ill-feelings towards Strauss himself. Pietersen in fact earned Strauss's gratitude for the selfless way in which he helped his captain to his hundred in the Lord's Test against Australia in the summer of 2009, despite having recently received an injection into his troublesome Achilles heel. Writing in his account of England's Ashes victory, Strauss commented: 'Pietersen showed what a team man he is, in contrast to some public perceptions, when ... I cut to wide third man on 97. The fielder at deep cover ... could not stop the ball cleanly. Sensing a third run, Pietersen ran to the danger end at full stretch, without a thought for his Achilles.'

Even though he had contributed to his own downfall as captain, it was hard not to feel sympathy for Pietersen as his game acquired some puzzling tics during an 18-month period that saw him score only one hundred in his next 22 Tests. That hundred came in the final Test of his first series under Strauss in the Caribbean, in circumstances in which England required quick runs ahead of a declaration; extemporising with sweeps and switch-hits, Pietersen raced to three figures off just 88 balls. It proved something of a one-off. His Achilles injury cut short his involvement in the Ashes series of 2009 and it was not until he played a starring role in England's triumph at the World Twenty20 in the West Indies in May 2010 that he relocated his best form. Twenty20 is a liberating format and Pietersen's carefree mood was probably reinforced by the arrival of his first child, Dylan, during the tournament. He hot-footed it to London to attend the birth, then returned to score runs in the semi-final and final, after which he was crowned player of the tournament.

Again, it proved harder to sustain peak form during regular life on the road. By August 2010, there was even some media speculation as to whether he should keep his place in the side ahead of the second of four Tests against Pakistan at Edgbaston. There he played an innings of 80 that was almost comically strewn with errors. Put up to speak to the press afterwards, he surprised many by attributing his loss of form directly to the loss of the captaincy, in conjuncture with his Achilles problem. '[It is hard] when you go from captaining a team to being back as one of the men being told what to do,' he said. 'It was hard the way everything happened . . . My confidence has obviously taken quite a big whack in the last eighteen months, what with having to give up the captaincy and then getting injured. I've just had to work hard and keep going.' Rather contradictorily, he added: 'It's easy to feel confident in that dressing-room. They're a great bunch of guys and so is the management team.' Had he spoken in such vein a year earlier, and said it had been a difficult six months since losing the captaincy, it might have elicited more understanding. But presenting it as 18 months of hurt probably prompted the reaction in many people of: 'Get over it . . .'

He was even less careful with his words a few weeks later after he was indeed dropped for the Twenty20s and one-day internationals with Pakistan, posting on Twitter: 'Done for rest of summer!! Man of the World Cup T20 and dropped from the T20 side too. It's a fuck up!!' He quickly removed the tweet but too late to spare him a fine from the ECB. This was the first public clash he had had with Flower since he had taken over as head coach (or team director, as the job title now was). By the time England had retained the Ashes in Australia for the first time since 1986-87, Pietersen was raising eyebrows further by claiming some of the credit for removing Moores, saying: 'We would not be here today if I had not done what I did. I got rid of the captaincy for the good of English cricket. There is no way in the world that we would have succeeded under that regime and won the Ashes again in Australia after twenty-four years.'

Such behaviour began to stretch the patience of the ECB, one source commenting to Steve James in 2011: 'His [Pietersen's] conduct ever since [losing the captaincy] has been terribly disappointing. He has allowed his showbiz friends to consistently convince him that he has been so badly wronged.' Prominent among those showbiz friends was Piers Morgan, a former editor of the *Daily Mirror* turned TV chat-show host in America. Morgan had long been a close friend of Pietersen's and Pietersen had once turned out for his cricket team in East Sussex in exchange for Morgan arranging a meeting with talent-show mogul Simon Cowell. To say Morgan lionised Pietersen would be an understatement: when he interviewed Pietersen for *GQ* magazine in late 2006, he described him as 'the rock star of world cricket ... when Pietersen comes to the crease, bars empty, women go trembly and kids go crazy. Behind the undeniably cocky exterior lies a very smart, fun-loving, generous guy ... A batting monster with a heart of gold.'

Even back then, Pietersen said that the thing that had changed most in his life since helping England to win the Ashes in 2005 was that he could no longer trust people. 'Things I've said get leaked and it's like, "Hang on a sec, how did that happen?" And you know how it happened. That's sad.'

Pietersen was quick to seal his new identity as an England player in the most permanent fashion, tattooing his arm with the Three Lions.

Michael Vaughan, Pietersen's first England captain and a long-time supporter, quickly recognised that his flamboyant star also 'needs a little bit of an arm round him'.

Pietersen's girlfriend Jessica Taylor watches on during the 2006-07 Ashes series with his parents Penny and Jannie Pietersen.

The Pietersen switch-hit was just one of his remarkable new innovations, seen here as he hits Paul Harris of South Africa for four in 2008.

Pietersen and Matt Prior collect their baggage at Johannesburg airport after the final leg of their journey to Zimbabwe in November 2004 was delayed. Both South African-born men would make their England debuts within a few days.

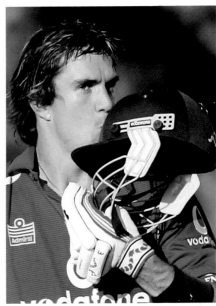

No mistaking the message as Pietersen kisses the England badge after scoring a century in the second ODI against South Africa in February 2005.

Pietersen plays his 'Flamingo' shot at The Oval against South Africa in 2008. It was another of his unique shots designed to knock bowlers out of their rhythm.

Pietersen launches Shane Warne into the stands during his Ashes-clinching innings at The Oval in 2005.

A big shot from Pietersen on his way to a rapid century for Nottinghamshire against Kent in August 2003, but his performance on the field was overshadowed by his comments off it.

The body language hints at a frosty relationship between captain Pietersen and England coach Peter Moores during the tour of India late in 2008. Both men would soon be out of their jobs.

Pietersen and Andrew Flintoff share a joke during the 2009 IPL when both men got a glimpse of the money on offer; for Pietersen this was to become a major issue.

Pietersen congratulates Andrew Strauss after the man who replaced him as England captain had scored a century against Australia at Lord's in 2009.

Pietersen is dropped during his scratchy innings of 80 against Pakistan at Edgbaston in August 2010. Somewhat surprisingly, he blamed his poor form partially on losing the captaincy 18 months earlier.

Pietersen watches on with Piers Morgan and Jeffrey Archer. His friendship with Morgan did not always impress others.

Pietersen walks off after falling to Abdur Razzak in Bangladesh in March 2010. His personal battle against left-arm spinners was not always acknowledged, but for a while he struggled to find a solution.

Pietersen takes the attack to Sunil Narine at Edgbaston in 2012, perhaps venting his frustration at missing out on the rest of the IPL season.

One of his great innings: Pietersen celebrates reaching his century against South Africa at Headingley in 2012. But the problems soon mounted . . .

Even at this early stage of his career in 2003, Pietersen was always impatient to get off the mark. His partners knew to stay alert.

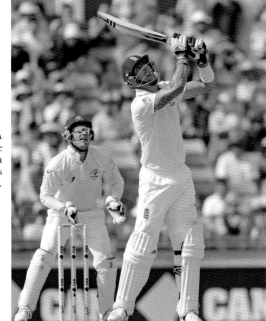

Pietersen hits out at the WACA in December 2013, only to be caught on the boundary – a dismissal that had the critics lining up to attack him.

After 'text-gate', Pietersen returned to the England fold in India, and seemed to patch up things with coach Andy Flower and the rest of the squad, but it was not to last.

A sorry Pietersen leaves the Sydney Cricket Ground wearing an England shirt for the last time. He was apparently 'disconnected', 'disengaged' and whistling as his side slumped to a 5-0 whitewash.

Meanwhile, Morgan never let up. Indeed, much to the infuriation of the ECB and England management, he went much further onto the offensive during the text scandal of 2012 and Pietersen's sacking in 2014.

Shane Warne, another long-standing friend, also heightened the friction between Pietersen and his masters by persistently using his role as a media commentator to attack Alastair Cook's captaincy during the 2013 Ashes series in England, and keeping up the criticism when the sides met again in Australia. Warne suggested Cook had little natural feel for the tactical nuances of the game and that England would be better off under Pietersen's leadership. It was doubtful if any of this actually helped Pietersen's cause, and while silencing Morgan and Warne must rank among life's tougher assignments, Pietersen himself perhaps could have done more to distance himself from these allies. But then perhaps when he thought back to the end of his captaincy he felt outnumbered.

And, right or wrong, Pietersen's sense that he had been hard done by over the captaincy possibly subsequently coloured his attitude towards the ECB and the England management when it came to negotiations over his involvement in the IPL. The die had been cast.

6

PIETERSEN AND LEFT-ARM SPIN

IT WAS during his post-captaincy malaise that Pietersen experienced the worst technical crisis of his career, perhaps the *only* serious technical crisis of his career. The Achilles injury that cut short his involvement in the Ashes series of 2009, and the troubles he experienced with the short ball in South Africa the following winter, were minor hiccoughs compared to what subsequently happened in Bangladesh early in 2010. There, what previously had been a little local difficulty against orthodox left-arm spinners – orthodox left-arm spin, for heaven's sake, wasn't that what Phil Tufnell had bowled? – became something much bigger, to the point where Pietersen seriously doubted himself for perhaps the one and only time. By his own admission, at one point he despaired of a solution.

At heart it was a technical problem, but it is a moot point whether it would have turned into such a full-blown crisis had it come at a different juncture of his career. Would it have happened, for instance, *before* his time as England captain? The post-captaincy Pietersen was a brooding, ultra-sensitive figure. Would the earlier Pietersen, swaggeringly magnificent and contemptuous of the notion that any bowler might contain him, have been so readily disarmed? It is true that Yuvraj Singh, himself a bristlingly powerful batsman, had already caused Pietersen some embarrassment with his occasional left-armers, but this was mainly in one-day cricket and was chiefly viewed as a pantomime diversion.

That Pietersen's problems occurred against Bangladesh, a team with no meaningful history as a Test match nation and no superstars, was of course relevant. Had it been Australia, he would have been in preparation-mode for weeks, if not months. Had he been about to face menacing fast bowlers, or Shane Warne's devilry, he would have left nothing to chance. But Bangladesh? Well, it seemed as though they were right down there with those coaches he didn't rate: they just didn't merit his attention, or his *respect*. And so the Lilliputians rose up and surprised their visiting Gulliver.

Pietersen, of course, was good enough to find an answer. But before producing conclusive proof of his genius by excoriating India's spin attack on the red soil of Mumbai in November 2012, the search for a solution took him on a rare journey that required him to admit that there was indeed an issue to be addressed. He had to concede his own fallibility. For a man who believed in the all-conquering power of confidence, and had wrapped himself in a cloak of self-belief all his adult life, this was quite a step to take. Not that he liked to admit it to the wider world. Once he thought the problem was solved, he was keen to pretend it had never existed. Reports of his difficulties against left-arm spin were, he suggested, unfair or exaggerated.

Speaking about his great innings of 186 in Mumbai in an interview with *All Out Cricket* in January 2014, he perhaps unwittingly alluded to the crucial ingredient in that performance: 'I play with such a carefree attitude that I'm not really fazed. If I get nought, I get nought.' Two years earlier in Bangladesh, he simply would have been unable to locate such a free-spirited approach. In the wake of the captaincy disappointment, he lost some of the bullet-hard self-belief that in earlier times enabled him to solve a problem much more quickly, if indeed he would have allowed it to arise in the first place.

The trouble originated with the introduction of the Decision Review System (DRS), which was designed to help achieve the best umpiring decisions with the aid of technology such as the ball-tracking device Hawkeye; this had the unintended consequence of forcing batsmen to play spin less with their pads for fear of being given LBW. It was a huge boon to spin bowlers, but for Pietersen, whose original method against left-arm spinners had been the traditional one of getting well forward with bat behind pad, it necessitated a serious re-think, as he explained in 2012 in one of his online 'Keep Calm and Smash It' coaching sessions: 'Technology has now brought a lot of umpires to give LBWs for batters that are defending straight and are a long way down the wicket. Five or so years ago you could defend straight, you could get hit on your pad out there, but the element of doubt was huge and the umpires weren't giving decisions. Because of Hawkeye . . . you are going to get given out.'

DRS was introduced in 2009 but was not used in every series – some teams were against using it and it was expensive to implement – but chopping and changing according to which regulations applied was hardly practical. By the time of the Bangladesh tour, Pietersen was still working through his best approach. His preferred solution of getting his bat out in front of his pad ran the danger of edging to the keeper or slip, or being bowled through the 'gate', and this was where he came unstuck against three Bangladeshi left-arm spinners: Shakib Al Hasan, Abdur Razzak and Mehrab Hossain. In the space of nine innings, they got him out seven times.

As Pietersen recounted to Andrew Flintoff, it was his third-ball dismissal to the 22-year-old Mehrab Hossain during a warm-up match ahead of the Tests that plunged him into what he described as 'the depths of despair'. By then he had already been out to Shakib twice and Razzak once in the ODI series without ever scoring more than 22. 'I went through three one-dayers in Bangladesh [and] got out three times poorly,' he said. '[I] just had no method. Then I went into a warm-up game before the Test matches . . . I literally did not have a clue. They had this little kid bowling spinners at me and I mean reputation-wise I should probably hit him for six every single ball. He bowled me a ball, I played and missed it. I played and missed the next one. I nicked the next one. I walked off the field, going, "Where am I going to go?" I did not know what on earth I was doing . . . I didn't know which side of the bat I was holding. I just literally couldn't hit the ball. I ended up walking out of a net and sitting on the [team] bus going, "Where the hell is my career going?"'

He had no choice but to battle through the Tests, which he actually did with some success, hitting cleanly through the off side before inconveniently being bowled by Razzak for 99. He was also out to Shakib in two of his three subsequent innings, so although he was making progress the problem was far from solved. 'I had to go back to the simplest form of batting in order to regain confidence in my ability,' he explained. He also knew that until he cracked the problem, it was not going to go away: 'I thought, "You know what, if they're going to keep going on it, maybe there is something I need to go and work on, maybe there is."'

Fortunately, straight after the Bangladesh tour, he was due to join Royal Challengers Bangalore in the Indian Premier League where one of his team-mates was Rahul Dravid, arguably the second best batsman ever produced by India after Sachin Tendulkar and one of the finest players of spin in the game. With Dravid's help, he worked out a plan. Dravid suggested Pietersen played more 'in-to-out' and focused on hitting the ball through the off side. As Pietersen explained in his online coaching advice about facing left-arm spin: 'I like to stay leg side [of the ball and] just close off the leg side completely and to just think [about scoring through] mid-off and extra cover, playing in nice straight lines [and] also keeping the bat face down real low with a low grip. You can take out short leg and silly point with a simple defensive mechanism.'

Sure enough this method served him much better and played a big part in ending his long run without a Test century, in Adelaide a few months later. Australia started the 2010-11 series by giving a first cap to the little-known Xavier Doherty, whose first-class wickets cost almost 50 apiece, in part because they hoped he might exploit Pietersen's weakness against slow left-arm (this was a mistake Australia committed again in the 2013 Ashes when they initially chose the uncapped Ashton Agar ahead of the more experienced off-spinner Nathan Lyon). Doherty hardly got to bowl at Pietersen in the first Test, but at Adelaide it was a very different story as England racked up over 600, with a sumptuous innings of 227 from Pietersen the centre-piece. From the 60 balls Doherty bowled at him, Pietersen scored 57 – the majority in front of the wicket through the off side – and it got to the stage where for much of the second half of England's innings Ricky Ponting dared not even bowl Doherty at the reinvigorated champion.

What was interesting was how after this emphatic response Pietersen sought to wipe from his mind all memory of his earlier trauma. Nasser Hussain, a former England captain turned commentator, interviewed him after the Adelaide match and was struck by what Hussain clearly regarded as Pietersen's rewriting of history. 'I could tell it had become a mental problem when I interviewed him after his double-hundred,' Hussain wrote in the *Daily Mail* in May 2011. 'I asked if he had proved he could play left-arm spin after taking Xavier

Doherty for big runs, but he quickly said it was never an issue. He was almost trying to hide it, [was] almost in denial.' Hussain felt that Pietersen was too gung-ho in adopting Dravid's advice; during the 2010 home season he had been stumped off Shakib's bowling in a Test in England, which was a very rare dismissal for him, and was generally too eager to get down the wicket and get leg side of the ball. His hands were coming down in an 'S' shape (something Hussain labelled 'scissor hands'), which broke one of Pietersen's cardinal rules of technique about always playing in straight lines. 'His brain became scrambled,' was Hussain's verdict.

In the first home Test of 2011 – so, a few months after Adelaide – Pietersen's problems duly resurfaced when he was LBW to Sri Lanka's left-armer Rangana Herath, getting into a horrible tangle against a quick slider. The umpire gave him not out, but Sri Lanka's DRS challenge was upheld after replays showed the ball hit pad fractionally ahead of bat. The following winter, during a Test series against Pakistan in the United Arab Emirates, he twice fell cheaply leg-before to Abdur Rehman, a left-armer who bowled a relentless flat wicket-to-wicket line rather than attempting to turn the ball big distances. Ironically, it was around this time that Pietersen produced his online video in which he firmly consigned his difficulties to the past, saying, 'Why I have been successful since I had my problems [is] . . .'

But better times lay ahead. Rehman could not prevent Pietersen scoring a career-best 130 in the last match of the ODI series that followed the Tests, and a few weeks later Herath was rendered powerless in a Test match in Colombo by a withering assault from Pietersen during what proved to be the first of three great centuries he scored during 2012. With Pietersen following up with an unbeaten 42 to finish off the game in double-quick time, he took 51 runs off the 52 balls he faced in the game from Herath, who perhaps paid the price for giving the ball more air than the likes of Rehman. Pietersen also had the advantage in the first innings of a good platform having already been laid: the score was 213 for two when he went in.

There is a strong case for considering Pietersen's innings in Mumbai the greatest of his career. First of all, it sealed his rehabilitation within the England dressing-room. Since the text scandal a few months earlier, the question on everyone's lips had been, 'Is Pietersen really worth the trouble?' This performance delivered an emphatic, 'Yes.' Then, in the first Test in Ahmedabad, another left-arm spinner, Pragyan Ojha, had left him looking foolish by bowling him in each innings. Pietersen had even conceded that he had been guilty of not trusting his defence: in the second innings he had abandoned his plan of staying leg side by going so far to the off that he was actually bowled round his legs *off stump* attempting a slog-sweep. England lost the match and when they then lost the toss in Mumbai on a pitch tailor-made for spin, their fate appeared sealed. But Pietersen served a reminder that he is never as dangerous as when the odds are stacked against him. Where he was frantic in Ahmedabad he was calm here, calculating the risks impeccably and, as his confidence returned, unleashing all manner of savagery on India's bewildered spinners.

He admitted that the sheer implausibility of success on such a pitch, against such an attack, seemed to free him up: 'On a wicket like that, where it was spinning as much as it was ... you sit there waiting to bat and you go, "If a ball's got your name on it, it's got your name on it" ... If I get nought, I get nought ... If you miss it and it hits your stumps, no problem. If you miss it, and it goes to the keeper, no problem. But if you hit it, it's *going.*' And quite a few of them went: from the 233 balls he faced, he hit 20 fours and four sixes. One boundary off Ojha, hit over extra cover with Ojha bowling over the wicket, he rated as one of the two best shots he had ever played (the other being the pull off Dale Steyn at Headingley three months earlier). 'Just the slowness of my bat speed through those balls is what stands out to me ... I do occasionally look at those and go, "How the hell did you do that?"'

Pietersen left many observers in Mumbai shaking their heads in wonderment. 'His innings ... was staggering in its range,' Simon Barnes wrote in *The Times.* 'This was no slog, for all that some of the shots were spectacular; this was no all-out assault, even though the speed at which he scored was stunning in the context of the state of the pitch and the match. He batted to a plan and yet left himself free to improvise, his mind at last free of clutter and worry ... The classic and the unconventional were blended into a masterpiece of an innings, extremes of approach integrated by his brilliance. A huge and masterful century on a turning track in India from a man who was supposed to have problems with spin, this was a colossal thing.'

Pietersen had been in danger of looking ordinary against a type of bowling that ought to have been bread and butter to him. In Mumbai, he cast that danger aside once and for all.

IF A VULNERABILITY to left-arm spin was a flaw that could be eradicated, another proved much less easy to smooth out. This wasn't so much a technical blemish as a chink in his psychological armour and it went close to the heart of the Pietersen Problem. It could have been called the Challenge of What Next.

The key to ensuring that Pietersen remained happy and performing well was – to paraphrase what he himself wrote in that notebook all those years ago – to 'keep it fucking interesting'. Like other gifted batsmen before him – Barry Richards and David Gower for example – he needed to find ways to remain stimulated. He needed tests to pass, and targets to chase, and perhaps this need became even more acute after he returned to the ranks following the loss of the England captaincy. Had he been a salesman on commission, he would have topped his company's charts every month, but no such obvious system of incentivisation was available. Alternatives had to be found.

This was a challenge not only for Pietersen but for those who managed him, and it was those coaches that understood him best who grasped this crucial point. Clive Rice constantly set Pietersen challenges during their two years together at Nottinghamshire, and continued to do so even after they officially stopped working together. It was Rice, rather than the then England coach Duncan Fletcher, who set Pietersen the goals he chased during the 2005 Ashes.

Just as the presence of specific goals was a positive thing, so their absence threatened to leave him disorientated. Without a specific aim in mind, Pietersen could lose his thread. This may explain why he was able to make 13 scores of 140 or more in Tests but converted only three of them into double-hundreds. As Andrew Strauss said of him: 'Even when he has a team on the ropes he can fall into the trap of entertaining the crowd instead of burying the opposition.' As Strauss also observed, if Pietersen had nothing left to prove, he lost his edge.

Ergo, give him something to prove.

Jason Gallian, who captained Pietersen at Nottinghamshire, was well aware of the conundrum. Early in the 2004 season – in other words, *after* Pietersen's falling out with Gallian the previous year – he saw how fiercely focused Pietersen could be when faced with a sufficiently interesting challenge. Nottinghamshire were due to play away to Hampshire, with Shane Warne in their line-up, and Gallian could only admire Pietersen as he started planning for this encounter two weeks out, plugging Stuart MacGill for information about his fellow Australian and which shots the best batsmen used against the champion leg-spinner. Sure enough, when the game came around, Pietersen faced Warne and did so well that, according to Gallian, 'Shane couldn't bowl at him ... he had to take himself off.' Pietersen scored 49 and Notts won in two days. 'You see those bits of brilliance and you think: how can you keep him going?' Gallian recalled. 'Once he's done it, what is the next stage for him? And if there is no next stage, then it becomes an issue. Once he's achieved it [a goal] ... it's very difficult to motivate him.'

Pietersen was actually highly stimulated for much of 2004 because he was getting near to qualifying for England and wanted to stake his claim for selection. Early in the year Ed Smith sat next to him on a flight to India at the start of an England A tour and listened bemused as Pietersen gave him a detailed breakdown of how he was going to play various South African bowlers. Smith recounted: '"But Kev," I eventually replied, "aren't we about to play in India?" "Yes," he replied, "but in a year's time I'll be on the full England tour to South Africa." There was something almost honourable about such unapologetically blunt ambition.'

In his early days with England, Pietersen was sufficiently enervated by the whole experience of playing international cricket that he did not appear to need any further motivation, but by the time Andy Flower took charge of the team, satisfying his needs had become a more complex problem. Flower seemed aware of this. In 2011, when Pietersen was apparently toying with giving up 50-over cricket and was overlooked when the England captaincy was split between Strauss (Tests), Alastair Cook (one-day internationals) and Stuart Broad (Twenty20s), Flower set him the task of becoming the world's best batsman. 'He may be disappointed not to be involved in the leadership team for the next few years but we are very keen for Kevin to become the leading batsman, not only in the English side but in world cricket,' Flower said. 'He is ambitious and an outstanding talent and could be one of if not the best batsman in the world. We want him to gain that status because that will help him feel fulfilled and help us win.'

Pietersen initially responded positively to the challenge. At the time, he was No.22 in the Test rankings but by the end of that summer had pushed himself up to No.8 after scoring heavily against Sri Lanka and India. However, after that he struggled to advance much further. He fleetingly went to No.7 after his great innings in Mumbai, but by the time of his final Test match in Sydney in January 2014 he had slipped to No.17. He fared even worse in ODI cricket. He was No.39 in the ODI rankings in May 2011 but subsequently never managed to get into the top 20. Overall during Flower's time in charge he never really came close to matching the heights of 2007, when he reached No.3 in the Test ratings and was the No.1 batsman in ODIs.

Becoming the world's best batsman was certainly an ambition of his in his early days but perhaps by 2011 he realised that such a position in the game was beyond him. Part of the problem was that however well he played there was no controlling how well other batsmen might perform, so perhaps the target was a little too vague to really stimulate him. Evidence suggests that it was targets that were difficult but attainable – say, scoring 500 runs in an Ashes series – which he really responded best to.

In the latter part of his England career, he rarely alluded to his place in the rankings and preferred to talk about his hopes of scoring 10,000 Test runs. This was a landmark he mentioned ahead of the 2013 Ashes series in England after he was recovering from a long lay-off with a knee injury and when questions were being asked about how long he might continue beyond the back-to-back Ashes encounters. His career tally stood at 7,499 at that point, which suggested he was contemplating continuing for three more years. He further stated ahead of the series in Australia that he wanted to give himself a chance to complete a set of home-and-away centuries against all major opponents by touring South Africa in 2015-16.

The trouble was that decisions over his future were not solely in his hands. The rancorous events of the summer of 2012 had raised questions in the minds of others about how long he should be allowed to continue in the England side.

7

PIETERSEN AND WANT VERSUS NEED

ONE OF the regular topics in Pietersen's early media interviews was how strict an upbringing he had. His church-going parents put great store by discipline and they were not so affluent – though his father was a director of an engineering company – that they could give their four boys everything they wanted. Pietersen said this was no hardship and believed it taught him some important life lessons. One was that if you were naughty, you were punished. Another was that you did not always have to have what you wanted: what you needed was different from what you wanted.

It would have been hard not to have been struck by the contradiction as Pietersen enthusiastically discussed with these same interviewers the things that his meteoric rise allowed him to buy (if indeed they weren't given for free by grateful sponsors). 'I can get what I want, when I want,' he told Rachel

Cooke of the *Observer* in an interview linked to promoting his autobiography in 2006. 'I'm still like a kid. I'll think, "Ooh, I want that," and if I can afford it I get it.' What was the most recent thing he wanted and got? 'My car ... I've always wanted a Porsche. One day, I rang Adam [Wheatley, his agent]. "Can you get me a Porsche, please?" I had a 911 within two or three days. I was in Pakistan at the time ... Or if I see a pair of trousers on TV. You think they're beautiful and you like them, you get them.'

While sharing a car ride with Pietersen between a bookstore and a radio studio, Cooke witnessed at first hand another example of his conspicuous consumption as he wolfed down a bag of Funny Face sweets his mother had just given him. She estimated that between the bottom of Tottenham Court Road and the top he put around a dozen of them into his mouth. I cannot do without them, he told her. When she asked him what his long-term ambition was, it took some chewing on a mauve Funny Face to help him answer. Cooke described his narrow mouth filling with lilac foam as he said, 'I want to be the best player in the world.' Having spent several hours in his company, Cooke's opinion was he was both difficult and charmless.

She was not alone in these kinds of views. The young Pietersen could make it very hard for people to like him, let alone love him, and some other journalists who beat a path to his door appeared to come away disappointed. Possibly his shameless materialism was what caused most consternation as he talked breezily into their microphones about clothes, cars and diamonds. While in one breath he spoke about how hard he worked for his success, in another he would describe how effortlessly at hand these items now were. The things that had come his way since the 2005 Ashes triumph were mind-boggling, he told Robert Crampton of *The Times* the following year. 'I get requests every day,' he said. 'Clothing, footwear, equipment, photo shoots. Some stuff is ridiculous money, you just can't refuse it.'

One of the things he definitely had not refused – how could you? – was £50,000 to wear diamond ear-rings during the 2005 Ashes. A big diamond was practically the first luxury item he bought after becoming an England player – he went shopping for one with Darren Gough in South Africa in 2004-05 – and by late 2006 he and girlfriend Jess Taylor, it appeared, had loads of them. He also loved clothes: he had more of those, he said, than he had cricket equipment. He had no trouble gaining access to the most exclusive restaurants.

Of course, all this only confirmed in the minds of the sceptics that he was not truly English. Anyone who was truly English would have been much more discreet about discussing what their success had brought them. Good grief, he would be talking about how much people earned next ...

'There's so many blokes [in county cricket] happy earning twenty, twenty-five grand, it's ridiculous,' he told Crampton. 'I never just wanted to earn twenty grand. I wanted to be the best player I could be and make a load of money out of cricket.' Crampton's conclusion was that, contrary to popular belief, Pietersen was not that bothered about fame. 'I think he's more interested in money.'

There were certainly aspects of fame that made him uneasy from the outset. His view was that he hadn't written an application to the newspapers asking to be a celebrity – he sought success, not celebrity – and found their interest disturbing and a little intimidating (give him Mitchell Johnson any day). Three nights after England won the Ashes in 2005, he emerged from a West End club with friends and was alarmed to find himself confronted by paparazzi (the club was a favoured haunt of celebrities). Their car was then tailed by photographers, prompting Pietersen to get out on Regent Street and tell his companions: 'You guys go home, you don't need this.'

He recounted to Paul Kimmage of the *Sunday Times* what happened next: 'I got out and stood in the middle of the road, trying to hail a taxi and the three cars that were following us stopped and they just kept snapping away at me. I was like, "What kind of picture are you trying to get here? Do you want me vomiting or with my finger up my nose? Are you trying to get me to give you the bird?" And they said, "We're just doing our job."' Pietersen got a cab and they followed him to his hotel and when he went shopping the next day they were still dogging him: he decided, 'That's enough.' He phoned his England teammate and friend Simon Jones and asked if he wanted to go to Los Angeles, where he had friends. 'I mean, who knows anything about cricket in the US, right?' So they went.

They got away from people who knew who they were, but Pietersen played into the hands of those who genuinely seemed to think he was only passing through cricket en route to Hollywood.

Memories of that night stayed with him and put him more on his guard, although he was confident there would be fewer such incidents after meeting Jess, presumably because she was better versed in which places were safe to visit and which weren't as regards photographers. Even so, he told Crampton that they had been twice caught by paparazzi, including once by a guy hiding in a fruit barrow in Manchester. As we have seen, they decided not to sell photographs of their wedding in December 2007.

It is worth remembering, of course, how young and impressionable Pietersen was at this stage of his career. He had shot to fame in a country he had moved to only a few years earlier and had earned the nation's gratitude for his part in regaining the Ashes after such a long wait. Riches, inevitably, came his way. In the space of a year, his world turned upside down. In later times, he would admit that he had done some stupid things with money, 'splashing out on flash cars' as he put it. Like a lot of people, once he started a family he took a more practical outlook. The money was still important – perhaps even *more* important – but he knew of more sensible ways to spend it, such as investing in property and the like.

But by then the die was cast. His rise to prominence was so miraculous, the way he played so unusual, and the story of his emigration so colourful, that it was very easy to label him (or perhaps mis-label him), and once those labels were attached it was hard to get them removed. He was a genius. He was difficult. He was a mercenary. He was selfish. He was a plastic Brit. Why would anyone bother to dig deeper when there was such a colourful back-story to regurgitate? Who cared if he was actually more complex?

His relationship with the media was a slippery beast that he never quite got to grips with. The trust was never quite there. In late 2006 he told one interviewer: 'I try to be the same person I was a year ago, this eccentric bloke who buys stupid clothes and diamonds. The only thing that's changed is trust. I don't trust anyone. People trying to stuff you, people trying to take advantage, things written about people I'm supposed to have slept with, one million percent lies.'

His interviews were rarely dull because he did not tend to hold back, but he came to realise that this was not helpful. 'It's not good for me,' he once said of his frankness. 'I get clattered.' In June 2008, he said (to an interviewer): 'I don't want to do interviews anymore because it just becomes a burden.'

He had recently given an interview to Celia Walden, the then girlfriend of Piers Morgan, for *Glamour*, a women's magazine, in which he had – in the spirit of the enterprise – provided some tongue-in-cheek answers to her questions. He said he sometimes cooked for Jess while naked and at one point referred to England as 'your nation, not mine'. Much to his irritation a tabloid newspaper picked up on his comments and treated them seriously.

He became even more reluctant to give interviews after the loss of the England captaincy, an episode which earned him unflattering headlines in some newspapers. 'DeTested' was the *Sun*'s verdict in a piece that described him as 'cricket's most hated man'. The notion peddled in some quarters that

Pietersen's attempted 'coup' against Peter Moores was widely rejected by his team-mates was never substantiated and indeed flatly contradicted by Andrew Strauss's evidence. This can only have added to his feelings of hurt and betrayal. At that point he had been writing a column with the *News of the World* for about three years, but the arrangement was to lapse. He was not the first big-name sports star to discover that those that built you up were eventually prepared to knock you down, but that did not make the shift any less palatable. And as Pietersen became less accessible, so those journalists who found him less cooperative grew less sympathetic.

As time went on, the relationship between the two parties might best be described as one of mutual suspicion.

THE ISSUE of what Pietersen wanted and what he needed was at the heart of his argument with the ECB in 2012. Early that year he transferred IPL franchises from Deccan Chargers to Delhi Daredevils on a significantly more lucrative contract. The Deccan deal, struck in 2011, had been worth $650,000 (though he never actually took the field for them because of a double hernia); at Delhi he was to be paid $2 million for a full season. Even for one of the best-paid cricketers in the world, this was serious cash. The catch was that the ECB would release him from his contract for only just over half the IPL season, and he would therefore receive just over half the money. To someone used to getting what he wanted, when he wanted, this must have felt like an almost intolerable imposition. Why couldn't he have all the Delhi money?

The ECB's hard-line stance was contentious. Players around the world were arguing for the international calendar to contain a window to accommodate the IPL, and most of the leading Test nations had in effect bowed to this wish in order to keep their stars happy. Only the governing boards of West Indies and England – the two teams whose domestic seasons most directly clashed with the IPL – attempted to maintain their traditional fixture lists and the issue was tearing the West Indies camp apart, with Chris Gayle, Dwayne Bravo and Kieron Pollard among others facing down their masters by putting the IPL first. There were, in truth, few England players capable of attracting serious attention from the franchises, but the ECB feared that by releasing Pietersen for a full IPL season it might trigger an exodus; it was also worried that putting out weakened teams might harm its broadcasting contracts. It warned of dire consequences for English cricket were it to relent in its opposition.

Could the issue have been handled more reasonably? Almost certainly. But the battle-lines over the IPL were not easily scratched from the dirt and it was Pietersen's misfortune to be caught in the middle of a power-struggle between the ECB and the Indian board (if only he had stayed in South Africa . . .). The Professional Cricketers' Association was in favour of an IPL window and sympathetic to his situation.

Again though, Pietersen's lips were working nothing like as well as his bat. Not long after arriving at Delhi Daredevils he bemoaned his situation in an interview to CNN-IBN. He described it as a 'big, big pity' that he was available for only some of the Daredevils' matches. 'I would love to play a full season,' he was quoted as saying. 'Unfortunately I've got other commitments ... I think there should be a window for the IPL because it is a magnificent tournament. There is a lot of money issues, that I think is what dampens it in England. People think that it is just a money-making racket for individuals, but so what? That's just the way it is. Sportsmen get paid. What are you going to do about it? ... It saddens me when I read negative publicity of the IPL in England.' He said there were world-class players in England who wanted to play IPL and it would benefit English cricket if they did. These comments were hardly likely to endear him to the ECB, but there was to be plenty more where that came from over the following weeks.

Michael Vaughan felt that keeping up a dialogue with Pietersen and keeping him away from microphones was an important part of managing him. 'I do think you need to be talking to him regularly,' he said on a BBC radio profile, *We Need to Talk About Kevin*, broadcast in September 2012. 'You have to get his response but don't let it get to the stage of him going to a media conference or interview, because you know that he's likely to say something to upset a few people. He is a person that you can manage quite easily if you keep it simple.' This may have been England's failing.

The tipping point for Pietersen was being hauled back from his season with Delhi – albeit to fulfil the commitments of a central contract to which he had put his signature – to play a Test series against a West Indies side whose own IPL players stayed in India to finish the IPL season. Sunil Narine even hot-footed it back, after bowling Kolkata Knight Riders to the IPL title, in time to play in the final Test in Birmingham. In Pietersen's absence, Delhi got to within one match of the IPL final and he probably reckoned that had he been there they and not Kolkata might have been champions. As if to reinforce the point, Pietersen absolutely shredded Narine's bowling in the Test match in a frenzied attack utterly out of keeping with a game heading for a watery draw.

Four days after the IPL finished, Pietersen suddenly and sensationally announced he was quitting international one-day and Twenty20 cricket. He actually only wanted to give up ODIs but his contract did not allow him to cherry-pick the short formats, another controversial move by the ECB designed to protect the less fashionable 50-over game. Again, how many players were really going to be giving up ODI cricket?

Pietersen's decision came partly out of frustration but was also perhaps a negotiating ploy: he knew that spectators liked to watch him bat and that there would be pressure on the ECB to relax its opposition to the IPL. Not all his public statements during this period were as clear as they might have been – don't put him in front of a microphone! – but what he was essentially seeking, it seemed, was time off from the international schedule to play more IPL, and specifically time off from England's two home Test matches against New Zealand 12 months hence in order to play a full season in the 2013 IPL.

But with the ECB showing no sign of giving ground, the situation was unchanged by early August going into the second

Test match of the South Africa series – except in one important respect. In the interim, a parody Twitter account was set up by a friend of Stuart Broad's which lampooned Pietersen's personality and was followed by a number of players. Unsurprisingly Pietersen wasn't too happy about this. Vaughan felt that when the IPL issue had surfaced earlier in the year, senior players in the team should have taken Pietersen out for dinner, told him to get his head straight and reminded him that they were a good team that had achieved a lot – they were top of the Test rankings at the time – and still had big things to achieve. 'You're doing things badly at the minute, chirp down, get out and play . . .' was the message he felt should have been delivered. Instead, it seems some players had actually gone the other way and enjoyed the mickey-taking. Broad later conceded that the team could have done more to support Pietersen in his battle with the ECB.

Then, as chance would have it – or perhaps it was not entirely chance because Pietersen always performed best when in a corner – he ended up twice at Headingley appearing in front of microphones with things to get off his chest. He spoke at the end of the third day's play after batting brilliantly for 149 and also at the end of the Test as man of the match. Inevitably, with only the final Test at Lord's to go before his existing England contract expired, speculation about his future was rife and his responses did nothing to dampen the fire. Starting his post-match press conference without waiting for Andrew Strauss, who as England captain was also due to speak, Pietersen indicated that he couldn't be sure the Lord's Test would not be his last and that it was tough being him playing for England. If he was hoping to elicit sympathy, the move was as clumsy as his attempt to get Peter Moores removed.

These remarks would have been enough to land him in trouble with his bosses – he had now been grumbling about the IPL throughout two Test series – but worse was to come within a few days with a newspaper report that he had sent SMS messages apparently disparaging Strauss to members of the South Africa opposition (South Africans he had got to know through the IPL, it might be noted). Short of support in the dressing-room and with the ECB, and largely friendless in the media, he was now seriously out of favour with the team management. His stock had never been so low and he knew he needed to do something to retrieve the situation.

He decided to reach for a microphone, and a camera, to post a video on YouTube in which he committed himself to England in all forms – effectively reversing his retirement of two months earlier – and withdrawing his plea to play a full season of IPL in 2013. It was an act as swift and surprising as his original decision to quit the short forms of the game in the first place, but predictably did him little good. His performance appeared stage-managed but above all his timing was terrible, the video appearing on the evening of Britain's 'Super Saturday' at the London Olympics when no one had time for a very well-paid sportsman trying to repair a crisis that originated in his wish to earn even more money.

After failing to deny the texts story, he was dropped from the Lord's Test.

Understandably, Pietersen's behaviour was viewed by the management as a serious betrayal of trust and, despite some face-to-face apologies, his future hung in the balance for several weeks. He conceded that he had sent 'provocative' texts and that he needed to rein himself in sometimes; the texts had been inappropriate and so had his remarks at the Headingley press conference. He was overlooked for the World Twenty20 in Sri Lanka and initially left out of the Test tour of India, before reconciliation was achieved and he was added to the squad. That other players may have been culpable in their behaviour may have played its part in the eventual decision to grant him a reprieve.

Puzzles remained though. A distinction was never properly drawn between Pietersen's two principal 'misdemeanours': the attempt to re-negotiate the terms of his contract, and the sending of the texts. The first issue raised serious questions which merited proper discussion between the ECB and PCA without the involvement of any one player, yet it got wholly lost amid the media frenzy over the texts 'scandal'. Then, a year later, the ECB quietly announced a schedule of home internationals for 2014 starting later than usual: the first match was to take place on 20 May while the first Test was not scheduled until 12 June, four weeks later than the previous year. By swapping the order around, so that the shorter-format games preceded the Tests, it clearly created scope for England players to spend more time at the IPL if necessary. Was this an admission that Pietersen had a point after all? It came too late to help him though; by the time of the 2014 season, England had sacked him.

And just how serious were the text messages Pietersen sent? Pietersen and the South African camp said that they contained only 'banter' and the ECB eventually accepted this. Outside this turbulent summer, when the IPL issue must have left them badly at odds, Pietersen and Strauss appeared to get on well, two fine batsmen who held each other in high regard. Strauss said of Pietersen: 'Nine-tenths of my time as England captain, I found him a good guy to have in my team. He set the right example in practice, and I felt he could have been far more resentful of me in the sense that he had been removed as captain before I took over.'

Even at around the height of his post-captaincy disenchantment, Pietersen told the *Daily Mail* in June 2010: 'Would I captain again? Andrew Strauss is such a good captain now I wouldn't even entertain the thought.' And in April 2014 he publicly regretted the texting episode: 'Andrew Strauss is a great friend. I was just in a bad space. We were not having a great relationship at that time. It should never have come out, all that nonsense. That wasn't a special time at all.'

Pietersen's subsequent relationship with the press was also intriguing. His return to the England team lasted around 15 months, yet he rarely spoke to print journalists in that time. Whether this was because he held the press partly accountable for what had happened, or it formed part of a deliberate policy to keep him away from microphones (and why would you not?), was unclear but it surely suited both him and the board. He was usually put up for press conferences only after a good batting performance or if he won a man of the match award. A rare exception was the eve of his 100th Test in Brisbane in November 2013, when he gave a sparkling performance, answering questions with good humour and even coming into the room carrying a copy of a local newspaper that had subjected him to a gratuitous attack.

However, his general reticence to appear did little to improve his relations with reporters who were only further irritated by his willingness to be interviewed on radio or TV by former players such as Darren Gough, Mark Nicholas and Andrew Flintoff. 'I don't read the media, especially in England . . . I have got no interest in what those gentlemen have got to say,' he said on arriving for the IPL in 2014.

Throughout the final, post-reintegration phase of his England career, he must have felt dissatisfied at his failure to tailor his central contract to his own needs. He had bid for something and been thwarted: he had found that he could not, after all, get what he wanted, when he wanted. It proved a fractious peace.

8

PIETERSEN AND EGO

PLAYING the ultra-attacking game that he did, Pietersen was always liable to lose his wicket in ways that would look foolish. He played thousands of shots in his England career, hit around a thousand fours and sixes, yet when he took on the deep fielder and failed to clear him, or misjudged a slog-sweep, or had his stumps splayed attempting an extravagant shot, he was likely to be slated as a reckless gambler and talent-squanderer. That was one category of offence. Another was his attitude when asked to explain the calculated risk that he'd miscalculated. 'That's the way I play,' he said after getting out in the nineties in a Test match. 'The hundred just wasn't meant to be. No dramas.' He must have explained how he got out by saying, 'That's the way I play,' dozens of times.

Such equanimity – such an apparent absence of *regret* – incensed his critics. Could he not admit that he had done something wrong? Pietersen's ability to quickly move on from a set-back rather than dwell on where it all went wrong (though he made an exception in the case of losing the England captaincy) was actually an asset, as it allowed him to play freely the next time he batted, but it was not appreciated by media men whose job it was to . . . well, look back and analyse where it all went wrong. After being quizzed in a press conference about his rationale behind a stroke that had brought a particularly ugly end to an innings, he said: 'You guys look a lot deeper into it than I do.'

This seeming to not care only fed the charge that he was arrogant and egocentric – too arrogant to be concerned about his errors ('There'll be more brilliance on the way from me soon, folks, don't worry') and too egocentric to appreciate the impact on the team of his mistakes. If his interests coincided with those of his side then happy days, but if they didn't then too bad . . . that was how the argument appeared to run. Pietersen's 'ego' – or 'egotism', as in an inflated sense of self-importance – was reckoned to be the cause of a lot that went wrong over the years: it was blamed for him wanting to get rid of Peter Moores, and was said to be at the heart of his troubles with England in 2012. Had his ego not been so rampant, had he been capable of more humility, he might have averaged 60 in Test cricket rather than 47 (or again so the theory went).

Pietersen's ego became a catch-all that covered a multitude of his sins, but essentially it meant to those sitting in judgement that he was irredeemably flawed and fated to repeat the same mistakes over and again. Australians were particularly fond of talking about Pietersen's ego (they came up with the nickname FIGJAM – 'Fuck I'm Good – Just Ask Me' – to encapsulate this), probably because deep down they feared what he might do to their bowlers, and it gave them hope that he might self-destruct. 'The Ego Has Landed' was the go-to headline to accompany a photograph of England's star batsman arriving at any local airport terminal Down Under. As a conversational playing card, Pietersen's ego trumped all others on the subject of why he wasn't better than he was.

But why wasn't he better than he was? Was it really to do with ego? Surely most world-class sportsmen are prone to egotism: it is what helps get them to the top in the first place. As Pietersen never tired of pointing out, confidence in sport is everything. There must be a fine line between believing in yourself and having an exaggerated sense of your own superiority. And which world-class sportsman did not love being the centre of attention? The big stage is supposed to be their natural playground.

Pietersen was certainly conscious of his status with the public as an A-list entertainer. When he (briefly) retired from ODI and Twenty20 cricket in 2012 he said, 'The saddest part is that spectators love to watch me.' And how could they not after the audacious way he saved The Oval Test of 2005, the most important match for English cricket in a generation? When Pietersen walked from the field at the end of that innings, Richie Benaud posed the perceptive question on TV commentary: 'What do you do next when you've played the innings of your life at the age of twenty-five?'

The inevitable temptation for Pietersen was to attempt variations on the theme, and to be fair to him he put in some pretty special efforts. Generally, he seemed torn as to whether to play to please the gallery. Andrew Strauss reckoned that he was sometimes guilty of attempting to entertain the public rather than crush the opposition, and got out as a result. This was not an uncommon problem for crowd-pleasing players, though. David Gower, another captivating stroke-maker from an earlier generation, wrote in his autobiography: 'I loved to see the ball fly to the boundary boards as much as everyone in the stands. There was a temptation to play to the image.'

However, I would argue that Pietersen's main problem was not an exaggerated sense of superiority – although he may have been guilty of that at times – but impatience. It was hotheadedness not egotism that was the root-cause of many of his most difficult moments. His judgement on the field of play may not have been flawless – whose is? – but off it he often responded rashly in the face of big decisions.

Take the following argumentative positions he adopted: 1) Were KwaZulu-Natal going to give him a fair crack in their first XI or not? Because if they were not, there was no way he was hanging around when he had an offer in his pocket to play for Nottinghamshire. 2) Were Nottinghamshire going to release him from his contract, or was he to call the lawyers? 3) Was the ECB going to remove Peter Moores as head coach or not, because as England captain he could not work with him a moment longer when everyone – literally everyone – knows that he (and all his back-room staff, for that matter) are not up to the job?

How likely, in all honesty, were these positions to bring about the result he wanted?

If you thought Pietersen batted in a hurry, his approach to tackling macro issues such as these was a whole lot quicker still. When he said he could get what he wanted, when he wanted, he seemed to mean he wanted it – however impractically – this instant. If his bosses weren't prepared to let him play in the IPL, well he would quit one-day international cricket straightaway and see if that made them think again, or he would use a press conference to tell everyone how hard it was being him and, no, he wouldn't be waiting for Strauss before doing so. His decision to un-retire from one-day cricket was no less hasty, seemingly coming in direct response to the fall-out from the texting scandal and with the hope that it would save his place in the team.

Was he afraid that it would seem weak if he consulted widely before deciding what to do on any big issue?

There were plenty of signs of impatience on the field too – the frenetic running between the wickets to get off the mark which kept both batting partners and opponents on their toes; the anxiety over hitting his first boundary. Once this was done, he could calm down and map out his innings in cooler fashion, but until then he could fret horribly. This was perhaps as much about nerves as impatience – the old thing about fear never being far from the surface – but the upshot was the same: for periods of play he could be a hindrance to himself and others. Over-eagerness was probably the cause, too, of the six catches he dropped (out of six) in his maiden Test series in 2005. For a man so meticulous in his preparation, he was nevertheless capable of jeopardising everything in a hare-brained moment.

Contrary to popular belief though, Pietersen was conscious of these shortcomings. He was often accused of lacking self-awareness, but in some respects he had a better understanding of his personality than many gave him credit for and with time he came to realise that impatience was a trait he could not tame. Towards the end of his England career, he even conceded that he would never quite achieve as much in Test cricket as he ought to have done because: 'I get myself out . . . all the time.' In effect he was saying that, yes, he was irredeemably flawed and fated to repeat the same mistakes over and over again.

Of course, this is not to say that he could not be patient. When he was playing at his best, and certainly when he was at his peak around 2006-08, he could be very measured in the way he went about constructing an innings, starting carefully and making sure he got an idea of the pitch and bowling before moving up through the gears. Even more than most players, he needed to get his eye in and his swing grooved before he could be confident of playing his shots safely; if he started aggressively, it was much less likely to last.

He actually worked very hard on developing patience in his early years, especially when he was trying to make the big scores in county cricket that would gain the attention of the England selectors. One of his most mature efforts was an unbeaten 254 for Nottinghamshire against Middlesex in 2002, when he had to deal with five or six men on the boundary in the later stages but refused to get frustrated. Even in this early period, though, his county team-mate Stuart MacGill saw boredom/frustration as one of Pietersen's biggest potential problems. After helping arrange a season for Pietersen at Sydney University in the winter of 2002-03, MacGill would phone up opposing sides and encourage them to set defensive fields, in a roundabout effort to get Pietersen to be more disciplined. MacGill judged the ploy a success when Pietersen finished the season as University's top run-scorer, but this was one particular puzzle that Pietersen would never fully crack. Throughout his career he was confronted by sides who reckoned that the best way to attack him was to defend. When they did this, it was often said they were playing on Pietersen's 'ego', but what they were actually testing was his patience. Many times it worked.

Twelve months into his Test career, when he was asked what he had learned most from his first year, Pietersen replied: 'Patience. That's the big one. There's so much time in a five-day game. I've learnt that particularly since [the tour of] India.' Pietersen failed to hit a hundred in the Tests in India in early 2006, falling for scores of 87 and 64, but started the home season with two big centuries against Sri Lanka. He even claimed early in his England career that he was philosophically predisposed to stay calm in moments of crisis. 'I never blow things out of proportion,' he told Paul Kimmage, 'because I believe what will be is what will be. That's something my religious upbringing has brought to me ... I can't control what's going to happen in ten minutes ... There is no point in stressing and straining. I believe my life has been planned.'

Of course, for a long time he was reluctant to admit to his

failings – no sportsman gains much by doing that – especially as one of the pillars of his game was a cast-iron self-belief. However, away from the spotlight he sought ways to manage and improve his mental approach. Along with team-mates, he worked with England team psychologist Dr Mark Bawden on understanding their competitive natures: some players were categorised 'assassins' (essentially, cool thinkers) while Pietersen was labelled a 'warrior', someone who was more emotional and aggressive in approach. These labels were not assigned in an attempt to change anyone into something they were not, but simply so that they better appreciated how their minds worked and, in the case of 'warriors' such as Pietersen, ensure that the emotional side of the brain did not disrupt the logical side. This field of study was popularised by Dr Steve Peters, who like Bawden worked with Britain's Olympians, in his book *The Chimp Paradox*, published in early 2012, which taught about mind management. Pietersen did not work with Peters, but said in April 2014 'that way of thinking works, I've used it for years'.

For all the accusations that Pietersen did not care how he got out, there was anecdotal evidence to suggest that he became as frustrated by his mistakes as anyone. In the summer of 2013 he said: 'It's just in-built in me to be aggressive and attacking. A lot of the time, I go, "What the hell did you do that for?" … When it [the shot] comes off it looks great but when it doesn't you look a complete mug.' He also described his switch-hit against Scott Styris in 2008 – which he appeared to execute perfectly – as 'stupid', because he had scored only 68 at the time and it could have got him out.

Then, in an interview with *All Out Cricket* magazine conducted shortly before the 2013-14 tour of Australia, he actually admitted to having an impatient personality. 'Because I've got this personality where I want things now, I'm actually quite an impatient person,' he said. 'I've actually not done myself a lot of favours when I've been batting. I should actually have many more hundreds . . . but that's just my impatience in trying to get to the milestone.' He then suggested that impatience was actually a problem he'd had earlier in his career – he put it down to 'exuberance of youth' – but had sorted it out 'in the last twelve to eighteen months'. The figures hardly supported this assertion. As has already been noted, he scored 15 hundreds in his first 45 Tests up to the end of 2008 and only eight in 59 Tests thereafter.

Perhaps his most revealing admission came during his BBC radio interview with Flintoff, when he appeared to concede that he was never going to fulfil his potential:

PIETERSEN: When I finish my career I want to go . . . did I do as well as I could? And I know that when I get to the end of my career, because of the way I play, I know I'm not going to have done as well as I could. I get myself out for twenty, thirty, forty, sixty, seventy all the time . . .

FLINTOFF: If you didn't play like that though, people wouldn't walk out of the bars and sit in the stands to watch you, you'd just be another player . . .

PIETERSEN: Yes, so I understand that. So that will probably be the little man on the shoulder that says, 'I think you've done okay . . .'

He seemed to be saying that, despite his best efforts, he was unable to change the way he played, that he was too old a dog to learn new tricks. When he said, as he often did, 'That's the way I play,' it was usually interpreted as a statement of defiance. But perhaps subconsciously what he actually meant was, 'That's the way I play. I wish I could change. But I can't.'

THE tipping point in the fortunes of Andy Flower's England, and to a degree the tipping point in Pietersen's international career, came when they reached No.1 in the Test rankings on a sunny afternoon in Birmingham in August 2011. Until then, pushing for the top spot had been the prime motivator for the team and everyone involved with them. It drove them to play an aggressive, attacking and highly successful brand of cricket. Forced against type for an English team to throw caution to the wind, they did it brilliantly.

Once the summit was scaled though, the outlook and approach changed. To an extent they had to. As Andrew Strauss pointed out, the hunters had become the hunted. Opponents analysed how England had become successful and worked on ways to deny them, in particular how to stifle a formidable batting line-up. In the 12 months up to the end of August 2011, England's top six racked up a mountain of runs; Alastair Cook, Jonathan Trott, Ian Bell and Pietersen made ten scores of 150 between them. England started to talk a good game about their aspirations to become one of the best England sides of all time but their actions were to tell a very different story. The side was very settled and everything they did suggested their main aim was actually to protect what they had got. They became more functional, more pragmatic and less instinctive. They were, after all, the hunted.

As chance would have it, they had to undertake a series of difficult tours away to Pakistan, Sri Lanka and India, but they did not help themselves by opting to play the home Tests of 2013 on slower, drier pitches than normal to exploit what they perceived to be their advantage in spin bowling: at the start of that year Graeme Swann appeared to be far superior to any slow bowler Australia possessed. This meant that England's batsmen spent the best part of two years grafting runs in conditions very different from those on which they conquered the world.

One of several things Flower's England lost sight of was the vital part Pietersen played in team dynamics. When he was batting well he not only scored fast but carried the belief of other players along with him. England's evolution into a serious team dated back to Pietersen's arrival and, although there had been times when other batsmen scored just as heavily, his sheer presence in the dressing-room, and the impact he *might* have on the game, altered the balance of power between England and their opponents. Pietersen needed good starts at the top of the innings on which to build, but he also needed to believe he had licence to play freely.

Probably a combination of circumstance and management decree meant that patience became England's watchword, even for their most notoriously impatient player. Post-2011, England started to play a brand of cricket that didn't suit their best player or, judging by the team's failure to total 400 once in 13 Tests between March 2013 and January 2014, anyone else.

Pietersen in 2012 produced three of his most explosive Test innings but they ran counter to the general tenor of the team's play. The first, in Colombo, was the most startling inasmuch as it followed a string of collective batting failures and four straight defeats; what it amounted to, in effect, was a unilateral break from team policy. Citing extreme heat as a reason why he felt he could not bat 'time', Pietersen explained: 'The only way for me to get a hundred was to score quickly. It was a conscious effort of attacking the spinners to get us into the game ... The only way we were going to win it was to play positively, play aggressively.'

Had it not been for his whirlwind efforts in Colombo, Leeds and Mumbai, Pietersen's strike-rate in the period after England reached No.1 would have fallen away even further than it did. His decline was nothing like as severe as it was for other batsmen though, as the following table illustrates:

Batsman	Strike-rate Jan 2009–Aug 2011	Strike-rate Aug 2011–Jan 2014
Alastair Cook	51.5	42.2
Cook's opening partner (various)	50.8	37.5
Jonathan Trott	48.5	46.2
Kevin Pietersen	61.4	58.7
Ian Bell	56.6	41.3
Matt Prior (keeper-batsman)	71.9	54.1

In the back-to-back Ashes series, Australia proved especially adept at capitalising on England's caution with some extraordinarily disciplined bowling, combined with inventive field-settings designed to cut off favoured scoring areas. Pietersen at various times was confronted with two short extra-covers or two short midwickets, and invited to try hitting through them. Twice in Australia he was caught at short mid-wicket as frustration got the better of him. Nathan Lyon's off-spin from round the wicket also proved an effective ploy, but his struggles were really the product of an entire attack giving away next to nothing. Peter Siddle took his wicket six times, Ryan Harris five and Lyon four. Pietersen coped far better with Mitchell Johnson's hostility and pace than most and was out to him only twice. That he passed 40 nine times but got beyond 71 only once illustrates how well they wore him down. It was noticeable, too, that the one time he really had Australia rattled was during a last-day run-chase at The Oval when he may have felt sufficiently liberated by the situation to bat in a way that felt most natural to him.

Three days after the Ashes were lost in Perth, I had coffee with Trent Woodhill, an Australian fielding and batting coach who had worked closely with Pietersen at Delhi Daredevils. Woodhill felt England needed to give more backing to Pietersen, who had taken a lot of flak for playing aggressively in the second innings at the WACA before holing out at long on attempting to clear the rope against Perth's famous breeze. This was a shot Pietersen had played successfully against Lyon during his hundred at Old Trafford, although he had since admitted he had only done so with some misgivings. He knew what a risky shot it was when the man was on the rope. 'If I was Andy Flower or Graham Gooch [England's then batting coach],' Woodhill said, 'I'd be saying to Kevin, "Mate, you've got four innings left, go out and take them on" . . . It's not been easy for KP, they've bowled well at him, but he's got to keep that intent to score . . . It's a case of reminding him who he is.'

But by this stage even Pietersen seemed to accept that 'playing the patience game' (as he called it) was the only way to go against such excellent bowling. 'I haven't found getting "in" the problem,' he said during an interview with Sky Sports TV during the next Test in Melbourne. 'Australia have bowled incredibly well and sometimes you have to accept that when international bowlers are on top of their game and [they have] an aggressive left-arm bowler who bowls very fast [Johnson], two right-arm seamers who knock out a trench on a length on off stump [Harris and Siddle], and an off-spinner [Lyon] who bowls a negative line on leg stump, you've got to try and play the patience game.'

In a comment that hinted at the demoralisation in the England camp, Pietersen referred to the difficulty of winning one Ashes series and then immediately being asked to do the same thing again. 'I've been told a number of post-Olympic athletes go into some sort of depression or negative frame of mind. I'm not saying we are in some sort of depression or negative frame of mind, but after you've competed at such a level, post that competition, mentally you are a bit fragile . . . to play an Ashes [series] and then another Ashes, and for us being away from home [the second time], it's a tough gig.'

The statistics showed that 2013 was the worst year of Pietersen's Test career – his average fell below 40 for the first time – but it was also Flower's worst since becoming England team director. If impatience was Pietersen's Achilles heel, didacticism was Flower's. In the wake of England's worst cricketing winter in living memory both men were to lose their jobs within days of each other, but there was a lot more to it than that.

9

PIETERSEN AND THE FALL

SPORT IS all about merit. If you are good enough, you get to play, and if you are really good there is nothing to stop you getting to the very top. That is sport's first rule, the rule of meritocracy. All the other rules of engagement bow to the principle of excellence and, by extension, when this fundamental rule is flouted it leads to trouble. When apartheid South Africa chose its cricket and rugby teams on the basis of colour first and merit second, it found itself ostracised by the world. When it subsequently imposed quotas in an effort to ensure than non-white groups *were* represented, it angered those like Pietersen who felt the system unfair. All he wanted was a meritocracy, because in a meritocracy he'd back himself to come top every time. The principle of fair selection is constantly held to account. The process of picking West Indies teams often aroused inter-island jealousies, with selectors accused (sometimes rightly) of favouring their own regions. In England it is customary to hear grumblings about the bias of selectors who appear keen to pick players at bigger or more fashionable clubs.

When England decided to terminate Pietersen's contract, and with it his international career, it jarred with many people because he had just finished the Ashes series in Australia as the team's leading run-scorer. This may not have been saying much – 294 runs at an average of less than 30 was hardly up to his usual standards – but nevertheless on a disastrous tour he had done better than the others. He had been an automatic selection for the Test side ever since his debut in 2005 and helped win four Ashes series. Statistically, he was one of England's most successful Test batsmen of all time, one of only six to have topped 8,000 runs, and in all international cricket across the three formats he had scored more runs for England than anyone else, ever. And if it came down to which England batsman spectators found best to watch, he'd have led the poll by a distance. The idea that he was not among the six best batsmen available to England was absurd.

Pietersen, therefore, was clearly being judged by other means, but what were these, and were they really so important that they trumped the merit argument?

In the immediate aftermath of his sacking, the England management struggled to articulate their position – there were said to be legal reasons behind the reticence, but this seemed more like convenient excuse than concrete fact – though with time it became clearer. There was, it was pretty evident, no smoking gun. Pietersen had not committed an unforgivable act that made his future in the team untenable. It was rather an accumulation of small things amounting to one overwhelming conclusion – at least in the minds of the men with the authority to do something about it – that the relationship between Pietersen and the team, or at least with certain key parts of it, had irretrievably broken down. Trust between the parties was gone.

A fullish explanation arrived on the day that Peter Moores was named England head coach for a second time, when Paul Downton spoke publicly for the first time since replacing Hugh Morris as managing director of England cricket. A former England wicketkeeper who retired from playing in the early 1990s, Downton subsequently had pursued a career in the City and been only loosely involved in cricket; as such he returned to the sport independent of past controversies involving Pietersen. He had no axe to grind, even if he may have taken soundings from some who did. Ultimately, it was his decision to axe Pietersen, as it was to reappoint Moores.

Downton had been in Australia towards the end of the Test series and what he said on the day Moores was unveiled was that he had never seen anybody so disconnected from what was going on as Pietersen in the final match. 'What you saw was a senior player who'd become disconnected from the team,' he said. 'I watched every ball of that Sydney Test match and I've never seen anybody so disengaged from what was going on. What you need from a senior player is backing and support, everybody working together, and we'd just got to a stage where that was no longer the case.' He said that he then spent two or three weeks speaking to coaches, the captain Alastair Cook and several senior players. 'We came to the unanimous conclusion that ... for the side to grow we had to invest in new players and build a new team with some core values. It was decided that that wouldn't happen with Kevin in the side. So we decided not to select him going forward . . . I don't see any intention of going back.'

England, it seems, got rid of Pietersen because they wanted to build a new team, with new players and new values, and they saw him – at 33 the oldest member of the dressing-room – as perhaps too set in his ways, too focused on squeezing the last commercial ounce out of his time as an international player, to buy into the cultural makeover. 'There are no specific issues,' Downton added. 'This is ten years of Kevin scoring very well for England but getting to a point where the balance shifted. During those ten years we had a strong side, strong leadership in terms of established captains and coaches, and that side could accommodate Kevin. That balance has shifted now and we've got to invest in new players, young players, and a new side won't accommodate Kevin. It's as simple as that. It's just to do with the balance of what's best for English cricket . . . The sooner we understand Kevin's had his time, the better.'

This was a plausible argument but one that could never be proven right. The management had set new parameters within which the players would operate and the management had decided that a disconnected, disengaged and ageing champion was incapable of respecting those parameters.

Downton did not leave it there, though. He revisited the topic at length a month later in a BBC radio interview with Jonathan Agnew during England's ODI series with Sri Lanka, a week before Pietersen was due to rejoin Surrey from the IPL.

His motive, he stated, was to reiterate that the decision had been taken in the best interests of English cricket. It was getting to the stage, though, where the more he said the less convincing the argument sounded, and the more he fanned the flames of the debate; also, as Pietersen himself pointed out, the timing was odd. Was not Pietersen the one who was supposed to make things worse when put in front of a microphone?

Downton stated that frustration had been the overwhelming reaction around the England camp to Pietersen's batting in Australia. 'He had a "This is the way I play" type attitude,' he said. 'I thought Michael Clarke played him like a schoolboy almost, in terms of, "Move the field here, move the field here, and – pop – out we get" ... Are you [Pietersen] really fighting it out for England? Clearly there was a feeling that Kevin wasn't engaged in the way that he should be.'

Was this really the best he could come up with: frustration at the 'This-is-the-way-I-play' attitude? Only someone who hadn't previously been involved with England during Pietersen's time could have put forward this dog-eared criticism with a straight face. In another amateurish phrase that aroused the ire of Pietersen supporters, Downton added: 'He was starting to play a little bit like a luxury player.' One of them on Twitter quickly invoked the words of Danny Blanchflower in respect of luxury players: 'Glenn Hoddle a luxury player? No, it's the bad players who are a luxury.'

More persuasively, Downton expanded on what his inquiries in the weeks following the Sydney Test had revealed: 'I talked to not every player but quite a few senior players and I couldn't find one supporter of, "We want Kevin to stay in the side" ... I and others in that dressing-room wanted people who were just purely focused on playing cricket for England ... The accusations made were that Kevin had too many different agendas, that he wasn't one hundred per cent focused on playing for England ... That in effect was the unanimous feeling about it ... the nearer the dressing-room you are, the more understandable the decision is.'

How deep Downton's researches went was unclear, but the lack of support was nevertheless damning for Pietersen. Mind you, as we know, Pietersen the non-collectivist was never going to win a popularity contest – and this, it seems, was what he was finally judged on.

Most eye-catching was Downton's assertion that Pietersen had sought the termination of his central contract. Asked by Agnew why the ECB had not explained its decision more thoroughly at the time, Downton said that the situation was complicated by lawyers for the two sides being in the process of organising a compromise agreement. This led to an information vacuum, although Downton conceded that he too was still coming to terms with his new job and knew little about social media (which became the conduit for anti-ECB sentiment). He said: 'We went to Kevin and said we're not going to select you for the World Cup [World Twenty20] and from that point on he was quite clear that he wanted to come to a settlement to terminate his central contract because we couldn't give him any guarantees in the summer either ... In the end his [legal] team pushed for that because we would have been quite happy to let the contract run out.'

Why did the ECB want to keep Pietersen to his contract?

With the IPL auction a week away, it was natural Pietersen would want to put himself forward for a full IPL season (and generally be a free agent for other work) if England were not minded to pick him again. Why not release him immediately? Not to do so looked vindictive.

Nor did Downton help his case by elaborating on the short-comings of the team as a whole in Australia. This merely raised the question as to why the failings of one player were held so resolutely against him while those of others could be explained away as part of a wider problem. 'That group of players had been together for a very long time, all of them maybe a little bit distracted in terms of commercial opportunities,' he said. 'We had such a settled group for so long it's very difficult not to become stale ... we just couldn't recreate that same sense of urgency ... the tanks were empty ... maybe as a collective the team got into a mindset where they felt they were better than they were ... maybe just all the success they'd had built what turned out to be a false cocoon around them.'

A response from Pietersen was inevitable and arrived the next day. For once it was measured and proportionate. On his website kevinpietersen.com (headed 'Kevin Pietersen MBE International Cricketer') he began by revealing – en passant – that it was at the ECB's insistence that confidentiality clauses were included in the settlement agreement (What was being protected? The ECB's reputation?). Given what Downton had said, Pietersen felt enti-tled to exercise his right to reply.

He wished to give some context to the cancellation of his contract: 'It was made very clear to me that I was not being selected for the World T20 squad, and the ECB did not try to give me the remotest confidence that I would be seriously considered for selection for England again. Had I allowed my contract to "wind down", as the ECB proposed, I would not only have forfeited the performance-related elements that are part of the England player remuneration, but more importantly my availability as a professional cricketer would have remained under the control of the ECB for a further eight months.'

As for his attitude during the Australia tour, he described the suggestion that he was 'uninterested' as 'wholly untrue'. His statement went on: 'Although I was having injections in my knee, which inhibited my mobility and thus my ability to field close to the wicket, I was fully motivated to play for England and while I accept that the series as a whole fell well below my own personal standards, I finished the series as the top scorer. I did, and continue to have a good relationship with most of the England players, which has been subsequently highlighted by a number of press interviews. With regard to the criticisms aimed at my "the way I play type attitude", I feel it's only reasonable to remind Mr Downton that this method has brought me over 13,500 runs for England, in addition to being part of four Ashes-winning teams and a World T20-winning side, all of which achievements I am hugely proud of.'

Touché.

Downton and the ECB subsequently apologised for his comments during the radio interview.

The idea of getting rid of your best player was not entirely novel. There were at least two precedents and instructively the context was the same as in the Pietersen case: teams that were struggling badly, men in charge who were desperate to turn things round, the urge to create a new togetherness with a pliable group of players. Homogeneity was in, individuality was out. Ageing champions sitting in the corner of the dressing-room grumbling about schoolmasterly bosses and driven more by personal gratification than collective pride, became one problem too many. Already different from their team-mates through ability, they now stood apart through disposition. For the management, it was not so much about whether they were good, but whether they were connected. Or that, at least, was the idea. In fact, both ended in failure.

In 1986, Somerset under the captaincy of Peter Roebuck responded to two years of miserable performances by sacking their overseas stars Viv Richards – the greatest batsman of his era – and Joel Garner, an act that had the predictable consequence of forcing the departure of Ian Botham. Richards was unsuited to playing in a mediocre team and had lost respect for those he was playing with. Garner's fitness was in decline. Botham had lost focus and was already talking to Worcestershire about a possible move. 'The whole culture of the county had become headstrong, loose and dark, and it showed in the conflicts we had,' Roebuck said. But his young side played little better once they were out of the shadow of the great men. They continued to languish in the bottom half of the table, Roebuck resigned in 1988 and the club did not win another trophy until 2001.

In an even closer parallel to the Pietersen case, England in 1992 dropped David Gower – their then leading all-time Test run-scorer – for a tour of India on which he might have been expected to do well, being an excellent player of spin. During the previous three years, Gower had been at odds with the captaincy of Graham Gooch, who along with team manager Mickey Stewart seemed to hold perspiration in much higher regard than inspiration.

During a team meeting on a tour of Australia, Gower had expressed some mild criticisms of the way the team was run that had not gone down well with his superiors. 'What really irked them was that I didn't particularly buy into the concept of being seen to try for the sake of being seen to try,' Gower wrote. 'They thought I was a bad influence on younger players who might prefer my methods to theirs ... To my mind running a team of sportsmen as a humourless dictatorship was not the best way to go.' Again, getting rid of Gower failed to bring about the desired change. England lost every Test in India and after seven defeats in eight matches Gooch resigned.

Pietersen, like Gower, was minded to say things that the management did not want to hear and, as was evident from earlier incidents, tended to say them in ways that hardly sweetened the pill. Before Downton presented his case, there had been media reports of a players' meeting after the fourth Test in Australia called by Cook and Matt Prior, his vice-captain, in which Pietersen was apparently heavily critical of Flower. Players agreed that they had become too dependent on Flower for direction, but Pietersen's views went further than that and were rejected by most, if not all. Two days later – New Year's Day – Cook told the team that they would be working on fitness rather than hold a net session, a highly unusual step two days out from a Test match. Cook's argument was that the players were not fit enough. Pietersen was probably not alone in doubting the wisdom of the idea but he challenged Cook, saying the players were fit and should be concentrating on their skills. Later that day, Flower, who had got to hear of what happened at the players' meeting, met with Pietersen.

These events provide some of the background to Pietersen's conduct during the final Test in Sydney, where he scored only three and six as England's batsmen collectively gave their worst batting display of the series. Should Downton – who did not allude to the players' meeting or its aftermath – really have been so surprised that he appeared 'disconnected' and 'disengaged' during this all-too-brief three-day game?

There was conflicting evidence as to how Pietersen got on with other players in Australia. One source confirmed Downton's claim that senior members of the team no longer wanted him, but Graeme Swann said that Pietersen was no trouble during the time he was on the tour (Swann suddenly retired ahead of the fourth Test), while Chris Tremlett saw him do nothing wrong. 'He was just honest about the set-up,' he said. 'It was a tough tour for everyone and naturally when you are losing things do go wrong and at times maybe communications did break down. If he thinks something, Kevin will just say it to your face ... he wasn't afraid to say what he thought.' Asked about dressing-room differences, Ian Bell said: 'To be honest nothing really happened. I wasn't aware of whatever happened behind closed doors – meetings and stuff.'

If past occasions when Pietersen played in losing teams was any guide, the issue of respect, or lack of it, may have resurfaced. As his former Hampshire team-mate Alan Mullally said: 'KP can be very black and white. His approach is, "If you can play, I'll respect you. If you can't, I won't."' Not many did much in Australia to show that they could play. Pietersen had always seemed to have trouble empathising with others. The story that he annoyed colleagues by whistling after his second-innings dismissal in Sydney showed how petty the arguments became, but perhaps also hinted at insensitivity on Pietersen's part to the wider situation.

As in the cases of Somerset in 1986 and Gower in 1992, Pietersen's sacking triggered a public outcry. Somerset members called a special meeting at Shepton Mallett where a vote of no confidence in the club's committee was held. Gower's exclusion from the India tour, along with the non-selections of Jack Russell and Ian Salisbury, prompted a revolt among MCC members led by Donald Trelford, a former editor of the *Observer*, who called for a no-confidence vote in the England selectors. In both instances, the motions were beaten but not before considerable embarrassment had been heaped upon those who made the original decisions. With Pietersen, it was another former newspaper editor, Piers Morgan, orchestrating the protests through social media rather than a formal vote. Morgan even got David Cameron, the prime minister, to agree that he had made 'quite a powerful argument' on Pietersen's behalf. But ultimately he was no more successful in getting the decision reversed than his predecessors.

If recent events suggested anything, it was that not only had England's star batsman become disconnected, but so too had the team and the men charged with running English cricket. The manner of the Ashes victory at home in 2013 generated little joy. It was hardly England's fault that Australia started the series so poorly that the fate of the urn was all but determined after two matches, but the pitches the hosts chose to play on militated against attacking, positive cricket. England won the series but they chose to win in laboured, utilitarian fashion, and when the players were caught urinating on the pitch during late-night celebrations at The Oval, it was easy for some to – in the words of Michael Atherton in *The Times* – paint the players 'as arrogant, drunk on success and out of touch'. Or, dare one say it, disconnected. Giles Clarke, the ECB chairman, even spoke to Flower before the Oval Test match about the apparent disconnection between the team and the supporters.

As the man orchestrating the wider tactical campaign, Flower must take a good deal of responsibility for this breakdown. Having farmed out the day-to-day running of the ODI and Twenty20 sides to Ashley Giles in late 2012, Flower had more time than ever to plan for the back-to-back Ashes campaigns, yet strategy became more, not less, confused. Cook's opening partner changed from series to series; fast bowlers were chosen because they were tall, not because they were any good; and key personnel were rested so often that Giles rarely got to see some of his best players. Downton likened the relationship between the two coaches and the players to parents whose children would gravitate to whichever one would give them the preferred decision. 'It just creates grey,' he said.

Flower knew he was approaching the end of his time with the England team, but the closer he got to the end the more detached his vision became. As things went from bad to worse in Australia, he seemed to fret most about the harm that was being done to the team's legacy, *his* legacy. His influence extended beyond his reign too: it appears he was involved in the two biggest decisions that followed, the sacking of Pietersen and the reappointment of Moores.

(It is a moot point as to whether Pietersen would have been sacked in the days before a coach became an international team's must-have accessory. Ever since Stewart was brought in following a number of ill-disciplined England tours in the early Eighties, one of the coach's primary functions has been ensuring good behaviour. Previously, dressing-room disputes were resolved by the players themselves, with force if necessary, rather as Chris Cairns dealt with Pietersen at Trent Bridge in 2003.)

As for the ECB, its handling of Pietersen's sacking was hardly public relations gold. Its original statement was short on detail and a subsequent press release focused more on 'uninformed and unwarranted criticism' of Cook and Prior following the decision than fleshing out the reasons behind it. Then Downton said too much, too unconvincingly. Giles Clarke effectively told the public to get over it. 'I'm confident the public will still support us,' he said. 'Sport is about regeneration and we have exciting young players in Jos Buttler, Eoin Morgan and Ben Stokes. They will empty the bars as much as anyone . . . Alastair Cook needs to stamp his authority [as captain] and I'm sure he will.'

Not everyone shared his faith. Neither Buttler nor Morgan started the 2014 season in a blaze of glory, while Stokes spent a lengthy period on the sidelines after breaking his wrist punching a dressing-room locker in frustration after getting out.

Stokes was exactly the sort of youngster the powers-that-be didn't want Pietersen leading astray, yet perhaps Stokes could have done with a little more of Pietersen's 'that's the way I play' philosophy after losing his wicket.

No one was going to admit how dysfunctional things were, but Peter Moores's comments on the day of his reappointment spoke volumes. While Downton condemned Pietersen for being disconnected, Moores indicated – unwittingly no doubt – that the disconnection extended beyond one discarded player. In fact, he made several references to the need to connect: 'I said this job is about connecting things ... If I've learnt anything it's been to try and help people connect ... I'd like to be involved with a team that's connected to the public [and] the media ... The responsibility of the coach and captain is to connect them [the players].'

But no one was any longer willing to connect with Pietersen.

IT WAS perhaps fitting that both houses in this falling-out had a plague visited upon them. Neither the England management nor Pietersen got out of it what they wanted.

The management and the board might have preferred it had they ended Pietersen's international career once and for all back in 2012. Then, there was little doubt as to who was in the wrong. Pietersen may have had a reasonable case over his wish to spend more time at the IPL, but there could be no condoning his sending of text messages to opposition players. He had breached the trust of his team. He was effectively suspended from one Test match and a World Twenty20 tournament for reasons which the public readily understood. When he next walked out to bat, in a one-day match for Surrey at Southampton, the crowd booed him to the wicket, and jeered him on his return following a first-ball duck. For these same reasons, it was vital to Pietersen that his England career did not stop there: his stock had plummeted, his reputation hung by a thread.

Eighteen months later, the argument had shifted, the mood was different. Pietersen had taken the opportunity presented to him after his reintegration to redeem his mistakes. He played an innings of utter genius in Mumbai that turned what had looked like a certain series defeat into a historic win. He also made important contributions towards the home series win over Australia. Although he underperformed in the return Ashes, England were by then a team in freefall, and everyone's credibility was on the line. His offences were unclear. His chief crime seemed to be what it had always been: the superstar who found it difficult to rub along with lesser mortals, who walked with his shoulder-blades touching so far was his chest stuck out, and who when he did speak tended to say more than was wise, if it was not plain rodomontade. Getting rid of him was a much harder 'sell' in 2014 than it would have been two years earlier. As Andrew Strauss wrote five days after his downfall, Pietersen was entitled to feel aggrieved at the timing of the decision. He could not have felt that after 'text-gate'.

By signing up to a fragile peace deal in 2012, the England management handed back the initiative to Pietersen. He gratefully took it.

If it was to be one or the other, Pietersen would have much preferred to be axed in February 2014. There was a lot of sympathy for his position, not only among vocal high-profile supporters such as Piers Morgan and Michael Vaughan, but also among many in the game as well as the public. Having seemingly not much considered how the story might play out, the management had turned him into a martyr. If they were slow to recognise this, he was not. He used Twitter to play the injured party to perfection. When an injury to Joe Root created a vacancy in England's Twenty20 side, he tweeted: 'Phone is on charge. Would hate to miss a phone call this evening seen [sic] as I don't have a voicemail!' Another time he posted: 'Phone just rang and it was a private number [excited] ... answered it and it was my mum! She said – "I'd pick you, darling" ... Grrrrr!' Then, hours before Peter Moores's reappointment was announced, he returned to Twitter to observe: 'Everyone Deserves a 2nd Chance!' followed by string of smiley faces and sad ones.

Within weeks, he had filled his calendar with a host of Twenty20 deals. He was to play for Surrey in the NatWest t20 Blast, for St Lucia Zouks in the Caribbean Premier League and the Melbourne Stars in Australia's Big Bash League, as well as in the IPL for Delhi Daredevils, whom it was announced he would captain. Financially, he was going to be doing better than he had with England, certainly an England side incapable of picking up its win bonuses.

Many thought this was exactly the outcome he wanted. If he was genuinely more interested in money than fame, he had surely reached paradise. But what he wanted, and what he actually needed, may not have been the same thing. As Chris Gayle found after falling out with the West Indies board and operating for a year only as a gun-for-hire, the novelty and the money paled soon enough. Nothing quite beats the meritocracy of Test cricket, the best playing the best in the ultimate form of the game. Make no mistake, Pietersen was hurt by England's decision to get rid of him, and his early games for Delhi Daredevils scarcely suggested he was comfortable with his new existence. He laboured for rhythm and found some horrendous ways to get out. Ten years earlier, his critics had dismissed his passion for English cricket as manufactured, but that was nothing compared to the plastic loyalties of the Indian franchises. He told one of his IPL press conferences that he hoped he might get another chance to play for England; had it not once been the other way round?

Pietersen's problems continued when he joined Surrey for the NatWest T20 Blast. Playing 11 innings over eight weeks of the group stage, he continued to find rhythm elusive and although he often got starts his best score was only 39. He headed off to the Caribbean to appear in two matches for St Lucia Zouks before returning for Twenty20 finals day, where a painstaking 13 typified Surrey's laboured semi-final defeat by Warwickshire. His struggles were partly of his own making however as he chose not to play in the county championship. If it was an understandable response to his ex-communication, it was also a mistake, and when there was belated talk of him turning out in four-day games in September, Surrey were the ones to scotch the plan. The club subsequently announced it was releasing him, indicating that if he was to return in 2015 he would need to show a broader commitment to the cause.

Had he played more often and scored more heavily, his claims that he wanted to represent England again might have sounded more realistic, and he could have severely embarrassed the ECB in the process as without him England badly struggled through the first half of the summer, losing across all three formats to Sri Lanka before going 1-0 down in the Test series to India (they later rallied to take the series 3-1). These events placed Cook, whose own form remained dire, under acute pressure. He came under fire not only from Pietersen supporters on social media but also former England captains, all of which only heightened tensions between the camps. This may have contributed to Andrew Strauss's uncharacteristic aside while commentating on a match to mark the bicentenary of the Lord's ground, a game in which Pietersen turned out for a Rest of the World XI. Thinking he was off-air during an ad break, Strauss referred to Pietersen as an 'absolute c**t', but the feed remained live to online viewers in Australia and the comment quickly went viral.

From the moment of his sacking, it was inevitable that Pietersen would have his say at some point, and it duly came with the publication of his autobiography within days of the expiry of the confidentiality period in October 2014. By choosing as his ghost-writer David Walsh of the *Sunday Times*, a journalist with an impeccable reputation, Pietersen's account gained an air of credibility it might otherwise have lacked. Walsh so colourfully and insistently ran with the main themes presented to him by Pietersen (picture a small nut being attacked by a large sledgehammer) that it was hard for the reader not to be persuaded of their veracity. However, sharp-eyed observers noted the inconsistency between what was a wholesale laying-to-waste of

Flower's regime and Pietersen's pronouncement in Australia that the dressing-room environment was the best he had known.

Strip out the hyperbole, though, and Pietersen's critique carried some persuasive points. The portrait of Flower, while overblown, chimed with the impression that the England team director became too defensive after England reached No.1 in 2011 and was no longer capable of pushing a team over-ripe on success to fresh heights. After all, Paul Downton himself had suggested the team had been too settled for too long and had gone stale, hardly a ringing endorsement of the man whose job it was to regenerate the players. It was also believable that Flower mistrusted Pietersen's risk-taking approach, which was diametrically opposed to Flower's own style of batting when he was a player: as Pietersen said, Flower was a grinder while he was a grandstander. The portrayal of Cook was sympathetic but almost more damning because of it: he was presented as a good company man who was too inarticulate to carry a team meeting; again, not unbelievable.

The most surprising and serious claim was that Matt Prior, the wicketkeeper, and senior bowlers – Graeme Swann and Stuart Broad to the fore – formed a bullying clique that dominated the dressing-room and demanded apologies of fielders who dropped catches. It was suggested that Prior – or 'the Big Cheese' as he was termed throughout – was a teacher's pet and playground bully, and Pietersen said that far from acting as a peace-maker during his own troubled summer of 2012, Prior had been someone with whom he had long had a difficult relationship. It was also asserted that Prior's dominating presence stifled Cook's leadership and Cook had fared better as captain when Prior dropped out of the team. The England camp came across as an ugly and dysfunctional place.

If Pietersen's aim was to entertain and shock with the pen as he had with the bat, he was not disappointed. The book was too one-track for most tastes – there was little description of the cricket – but as a dissection of dressing-room dynamics it made compelling reading. While Pietersen drove home his message with a string of media interviews, the ECB's response was muted and feeble. A document listing Pietersen's supposed misdemeanours in Australia mysteriously surfaced around the time the book appeared, but many may have found the charges as unconvincing as the board's denials that it had had any part in the document entering the public domain.

No ECB official stepped forward to repudiate Pietersen's version and it was eventually left to Cook, apparently acting on his own initiative, to do so in an interview with BBC. Clearly shocked at the level of vitriol, Cook said Pietersen had tarnished a great era for English cricket with his claims. He did, however, tacitly acknowledge the existence of the bullying issue, although he did not call it that. 'Frustrations probably boiled over more than they should have done,' he said. 'Did it overstep the mark a couple of times? Possibly, but we addressed those issues.'

If publication of the book handed him a small victory, Pietersen undoubtedly lost the overall war. Whatever slim chance he thought he had of playing for England again had now vanished. Once again, he had acted in hot blood and by doing so denied himself the thing he said he wanted. Short-term satisfaction in the hasty telling of his side of the story was surely going to give way to long-term repentance as England continued to play on without him. And with Joe Root, Gary Ballance and Moeen Ali scoring seven hundreds between them in the home Tests against Sri Lanka and India, a new middle-order batting line-up was already taking shape. Pietersen's release by Delhi Daredevils a few weeks later only reinforced the impression of a man running out of friends.

There was no time for the ECB or Cook to gloat. After yet another series defeat in Sri Lanka, the England selectors finally accepted that they could no longer shore up Cook and sacked him as one-day captain. Without a hundred in 59 international innings, his position had become almost untenable, but having been steadfastly backed by the board ever since Pietersen's sacking he was devastated to find the axe had now fallen on him only six weeks away from a World Cup.

How good Pietersen would have been had he been allowed to continue with England is a tricky question. His right knee caused him a lot of trouble in the first half of 2013, cutting short his New Zealand tour and forcing him to flirt with surgery, and it was still a problem in Australia. In the period since his recall in October 2012, he had averaged 36 in Tests and 28 in one-day internationals, which suggests he was no longer quite the player he once was. But not many would have bet against him producing a handful of magical performances. As was often said, he may not have been a great player but he was a player of great innings. He was also without doubt one of cricket's greatest entertainers. This, rather than all the controversy, and the bitterness of his split with England, should be his final epitaph.

KEVIN PIETERSEN'S CAREER RECORD

STATISTICS COMPILED BY IAN MARSHALL

(ALL FIGURES CORRECT TO 13 FEBRUARY 2015)

FACTFILE

Kevin Peter Pietersen, born Pietermaritzburg, South Africa, 27 June 1980

Education: Maritzburg College; Natal University

Height: 6′4″

First-class teams: Natal/KwaZulu-Natal 1997-98 to 1999-00; Nottinghamshire 2001-04, cap 2002; Hampshire 2005-10, cap 2005; Surrey 2010 to date; Dolphins 2010-11

Wisden Cricketer of the Year 2005

MBE 2006

Test debut: England v Australia, at Lord's, 21-4 July 2005, scoring 57 and 64*

One-day international debut: England v Zimbabwe, at Harare, 28 November 2004, scoring 27*

Twenty20 international debut: England v Australia, at Southampton, 13 June 2005, scoring 34

First-class debut: Natal B v Easterns, at Durban, 6-8 March 1998, scoring 3*

Limited-overs debut: KwaZulu-Natal v Border, at East London, 29 January 1999, did not bat

Twenty20 debut: Nottinghamshire v Durham, at Chester-le-Street, 13 June 2003, scoring 25

MATCH-BY-MATCH TEST RECORD

Test	Opponent	Venue	Date	1st Inns	How out	2nd Inns	How out	Result
1	Australia	Lord's	21-Jul-05	57	Ct Warne	64	Not Out	Lost 239
2	Australia	Birmingham	04-Aug-05	71	Ct Lee	20	Ct Warne	Won 2
3	Australia	Manchester	11-Aug-05	21	Ct Lee	0	LBW McGrath	Drawn
4	Australia	Nottingham	25-Aug-05	45	Ct Lee	23	Ct Lee	Won 3w
5	Australia	The Oval	08-Sep-05	14	B Warne	158	B McGrath	Drawn
6	Pakistan	Multan	12-Nov-05	5	Ct Kaneria	19	Ct Sami	Lost 22
7	Pakistan	Faisalabad	20-Nov-05	100	Ct Shoaib	42	Ct Naved	Drawn
8	Pakistan	Lahore	29-Nov-05	34	Ct Naved	1	Ct Kaneria	Lost I/100
9	India	Nagpur	01-Mar-06	15	B Sreesanth	87	Ct Kumble	Drawn
10	India	Mohali	09-Mar-06	64	Ct Patel	4	Ct Harbhajan	Lost 9w
11	India	Mumbai	18-Mar-06	39	Ct Sreesanth	7	Ct Kumble	Won 212
12	Sri Lanka	Lord's	11-May-06	158	LBW Vaas	DNB		Drawn
13	Sri Lanka	Birmingham	25-May-06	142	LBW Muralitharan	13	LBW Muralitharan	Won 6w
14	Sri Lanka	Nottingham	02-Jun-06	41	Ct Muralitharan	6	Ct Muralitharan	Lost 134
15	Pakistan	Lord's	13-Jul-06	21	LBW Razzaq	41	St Afridi	Drawn
16	Pakistan	Manchester	27-Jul-06	38	Ct Gul	DNB		Won I/120
17	Pakistan	Leeds	04-Aug-06	135	Ct Sami	16	B Kaneria	Won 167
18	Pakistan	The Oval	17-Aug-06	0	Ct Asif	96	Ct Nazir	Won (concession)
19	Australia	Brisbane	23-Nov-06	16	LBW McGrath	92	Ct Lee	Lost 277
20	Australia	Adelaide	01-Dec-06	158	Run Out	2	B Warne	Lost 6w
21	Australia	Perth	14-Dec-06	70	Ct Lee	60	Not Out	Lost 206

Test	Opponent	Venue	Date	1st Inns	How out	2nd Inns	How out	Result
22	Australia	Melbourne	26-Dec-06	21	Ct Warne	1	B Clark	Lost I/99
23	Australia	Sydney	02-Jan-07	41	Ct McGrath	29	Ct McGrath	Lost 10w
24	West Indies	Lord's	17-May-07	26	Ct Collymore	109	LBW Gayle	Drawn
25	West Indies	Leeds	25-May-07	226	Ct Bravo	DNB		Won I/283
26	West Indies	Manchester	07-Jun-07	9	Ct Collymore	68	Hit Wkt Bravo	Won 60
27	West Indies	Chester-le-Street	15-Jun-07	0	Ct Edwards	28	Ct Gayle	Won 7w
28	India	Lord's	19-Jul-07	37	Ct Khan	134	B Singh	Drawn
29	India	Nottingham	27-Jul-07	13	LBW Singh	19	LBW Singh	Lost 7w
30	India	The Oval	09-Aug-07	41	Ct Tendulkar	101	Ct Sreesanth	Drawn
31	Sri Lanka	Kandy	01-Dec-07	31	LBW Muralitharan	18	B Fernando	Lost 88
32	Sri Lanka	Colombo, SSC	09-Dec-07	1	Ct Vaas	45	Not Out	Drawn
33	Sri Lanka	Galle	18-Dec-07	1	Ct Malinga	30	Ct Muralitharan	Drawn
34	New Zealand	Hamilton	05-Mar-08	42	Ct Vettori	6	LBW Mills	Lost 189
35	New Zealand	Wellington	13-Mar-08	31	B Gillespie	17	Run Out	Won 126
36	New Zealand	Napier	22-Mar-08	129	Ct Southee	34	Ct Vettori	Won 121
37	New Zealand	Lord's	15-May-08	3	LBW Vettori	DNB		Drawn
38	New Zealand	Manchester	23-May-08	26	Ct Vettori	42	Run Out	Won 6w
39	New Zealand	Nottingham	05-Jun-08	115	Ct O'Brien	DNB		Won I/9
40	South Africa	Lord's	10-Jul-08	152	Ct Morkel	DNB		Drawn
41	South Africa	Leeds	18-Jul-08	45	Ct Steyn	13	Ct Kallis	Lost 10w
42	South Africa	Birmingham	30-Jul-08	4	Ct Kallis	94	Ct Harris	Lost 5w

Test	Opponent	Venue	Date	1st Inns	How out	2nd Inns	How out	Result
43	South Africa	The Oval	07-Aug-08	100	Ct Ntini	13	Ct Harris	Won 6w
44	India	Chennai	11-Dec-08	4	Ct Khan	1	LBW Yuvraj	Lost 6w
45	India	Mohali	19-Dec-08	144	LBW Harbhajan	DNB		Drawn
46	West Indies	Kingston	04-Feb-09	97	Ct Benn	1	B Taylor	Lost 1/23
47	West Indies	North Sound	13-Feb-09	DNB		DNB		Drawn (abandoned)
48	West Indies	St John's	15-Feb-09	51	B Taylor	32	Ct Benn	Drawn
49	West Indies	Bridgetown	26-Feb-09	41	LBW Edwards	72	Not Out	Drawn
50	West Indies	Port of Spain	06-Mar-09	10	B Hinds	102	Ct Edwards	Drawn
51	West Indies	Lord's	06-May-09	0	Ct Edwards	DNB		Won 10w
52	West Indies	Chester-le-Street	14-May-09	49	Ct Benn	DNB		Won 1/83
53	Australia	Cardiff	08-Jul-09	69	Ct Hauritz	8	B Hilfenhaus	Drawn
54	Australia	Lord's	16-Jul-09	32	Ct Siddle	44	Ct Siddle	Won 115
55	South Africa	Centurion	16-Dec-09	40	B Morkel	81	Run Out	Drawn
56	South Africa	Durban	26-Dec-09	31	LBW Harris	DNB		Won 1/98
57	South Africa	Cape Town	03-Jan-10	0	Ct Steyn	6	LBW Steyn	Drawn
58	South Africa	Johannesburg	14-Jan-10	7	Ct Morkel	12	Ct Parnell	Lost 1/74
59	Bangladesh	Chittagong	12-Mar-10	99	B Razzak	32	LBW Shakib	Won 181
60	Bangladesh	Mirpur	20-Mar-10	45	Ct Shakib	74	Not Out	Won 9w
61	Bangladesh	Lord's	27-May-10	18	B Shakib	10	Not Out	Won 8w
62	Bangladesh	Manchester	04-Jun-10	64	St Shakib	DNB		Won 1/80
63	Pakistan	Nottingham	29-Jul-10	9	B Asif	22	Ct Gul	Won 354

Test	Opponent	Venue	Date	1st Inns	How out	2nd Inns	How out	Result
64	Pakistan	Birmingham	06-Aug-10	80	Ct Ajmal	DNB		Won 9w
65	Pakistan	The Oval	18-Aug-10	6	Ct Riaz	23	B Ajmal	Lost 4w
66	Pakistan	Lord's	26-Aug-10	0	Ct Aamer	DNB		Won 1/225
67	Australia	Brisbane	25-Nov-10	43	Ct Siddle	DNB		Drawn
68	Australia	Adelaide	03-Dec-10	227	Ct Doherty	DNB		Won 1/71
69	Australia	Perth	16-Dec-10	0	LBW Johnson	3	Ct Hilfenhaus	Lost 267
70	Australia	Melbourne	26-Dec-10	51	LBW Siddle	DNB		Won 1/157
71	Australia	Sydney	03-Jan-11	36	Ct Johnson	DNB		Won 1/83
72	Sri Lanka	Cardiff	26-May-11	3	LBW Herath	DNB		Won 1/14
73	Sri Lanka	Lord's	03-Jun-11	2	Ct Lakmal	72	B Herath	Drawn
74	Sri Lanka	Southampton	16-Jun-11	85	Ct Perera	DNB		Drawn
75	India	Lord's	21-Jul-11	202	Not Out	1	Ct Sharma	Won 196
76	India	Nottingham	29-Jul-11	29	Ct Sreesanth	63	Ct Sreesanth	Won 319
77	India	Birmingham	10-Aug-11	63	LBW Kumar	DNB		Won 1/242
78	India	The Oval	18-Aug-11	175	Ct Raina	DNB		Won 1/8
79	Pakistan	Dubai	17-Jan-12	2	LBW Ajmal	0	Ct Gul	Lost 10w
80	Pakistan	Abu Dhabi	25-Jan-12	14	Ct Ajmal	1	LBW Rehman	Lost 72
81	Pakistan	Dubai	03-Feb-12	32	LBW Rehman	18	B Ajmal	Lost 71
82	Sri Lanka	Galle	26-Mar-12	3	B Welagedara	30	Ct Kaluhalamulla	Lost 75
83	Sri Lanka	Colombo, PSS	03-Apr-12	151	LBW Herath	42	Not Out	Won 8w
84	West Indies	Lord's	17-May-12	32	Ct Samuels	13	Ct Gabriel	Won 5w

Test	Opponent	Venue	Date	1st Inns	How out	2nd Inns	How out	Result
85	West Indies	Nottingham	25-May-12	80	LBW Rampaul	DNB		Won 9w
86	West Indies	Birmingham	07-Jun-12	78	Ct Samuels	DNB		Drawn
87	South Africa	The Oval	19-Jul-12	42	Ct Kallis	16	B Morkel	Lost I/12
88	South Africa	Leeds	02-Aug-12	149	LBW Morkel	12	Ct Philander	Drawn
89	India	Ahmedabad	15-Nov-12	17	B Ojha	2	B Ojha	Lost 9w
90	India	Mumbai	23-Nov-12	186	Ct Ojha	DNB		Won 10w
91	India	Kolkata	05-Dec-12	54	LBW Ashwin	0	Ct Ashwin	Won 7w
92	India	Nagpur	13-Dec-12	73	Ct Jadeja	6	B Jadeja	Drawn
93	New Zealand	Dunedin	06-Mar-13	0	LBW Wagner	12	Ct Wagner	Drawn
94	New Zealand	Wellington	14-Mar-13	73	Ct Martin	DNB		Drawn
95	Australia	Nottingham	10-Jul-13	14	Ct Siddle	64	B Pattinson	Won 14
96	Australia	Lord's	18-Jul-13	2	Ct Harris	5	Ct Siddle	Won 347
97	Australia	Manchester	01-Aug-13	113	LBW Starc	8	Ct Siddle	Drawn
98	Australia	Chester-le-Street	09-Aug-13	26	Ct Lyon	44	Ct Lyon	Won 74
99	Australia	The Oval	21-Aug-13	50	Ct Starc	62	Ct Harris	Drawn
100	Australia	Brisbane	21-Nov-13	18	Ct Harris	26	Ct Johnson	Lost 381
101	Australia	Adelaide	05-Dec-13	4	Ct Siddle	53	B Siddle	Lost 218
102	Australia	Perth	13-Dec-13	19	Ct Siddle	45	Ct Lyon	Lost 150
103	Australia	Melbourne	26-Dec-13	71	B Johnson	49	Ct Lyon	Lost 8w
104	Australia	Sydney	03-Jan-14	3	Ct Harris	6	Ct Harris	Lost 281

TEST MATCH AVERAGES BATTING AND FIELDING

Opponent	M	I	NO	HS	Runs	Ave	100	50	Ct
Australia	27	50	2	227	2158	44.95	4	13	17
India	16	28	1	202*	1581	58.55	6	6	9
West Indies	14	21	1	226	1124	56.20	3	6	4
Sri Lanka	11	19	2	158	874	51.41	3	2	9
South Africa	10	18	-	152	817	45.38	3	2	2
Pakistan	14	25	-	135	755	30.20	2	2	12
New Zealand	8	13	-	129	530	40.76	2	1	7
Bangladesh	4	7	2	99	342	68.40	-	3	2
Overall	**104**	**181**	**8**	**227**	**8181**	**47.28**	**23**	**35**	**62**

TEST CENTURIES

Score	Balls	Fours	Sixes	Opponent	Venue	Date
227	308	33	1	Australia	Adelaide	2010-11
226	262	24	2	West Indies	Leeds	2007
202*	326	21	1	India	Lord's	2011
186	233	20	4	India	Mumbai	2012-13
175	232	27	-	India	The Oval	2011
158	187	15	7	Australia	The Oval	2005
158	205	19	2	Sri Lanka	Lord's	2006
158	257	15	1	Australia	Adelaide	2006-07
152	181	20	1	South Africa	Lord's	2008
151	165	16	6	Sri Lanka	Colombo, PSS	2011-12
149	214	22	1	South Africa	Leeds	2012
144	201	17	1	India	Mohali	2008-09
142	157	20	3	Sri Lanka	Birmingham	2006
135	169	20	2	Pakistan	Leeds	2006
134	213	14	1	India	Lord's	2007
129	208	12	1	New Zealand	Napier	2007-08
115	223	14	-	New Zealand	Nottingham	2008
113	206	12	2	Australia	Manchester	2013
109	138	12	-	West Indies	Lord's	2007
102	92	9	1	West Indies	Port of Spain	2008-09
101	159	18	-	India	The Oval	2007
100	137	6	3	Pakistan	Faisalabad	2005-06
100	137	15	-	South Africa	The Oval	2008

MOST SUCCESSFUL BOWLERS AGAINST PIETERSEN

10	P.M.Siddle	Australia
6	B.Lee	Australia
6	M.Muralitharan	Sri Lanka
5	R.J.Harris	Australia
5	G.D.McGrath	Australia
5	M.Morkel	South Africa
5	Saeed Ajmal	Pakistan
5	S.Sreesanth	India
5	S.K.Warne	Australia

7000 TEST RUNS FOR ENGLAND

	M	I	NO	HS	Runs	Ave	100	50
G.A.Gooch	118	215	6	333	8900	42.58	20	46
A.J.Stewart	133	235	21	190	8463	39.54	15	45
A.N.Cook	109	194	11	294	8423	46.02	25	38
D.I.Gower	117	204	18	215	8231	44.25	18	39
K.P.Pietersen	**104**	**181**	**8**	**227**	**8181**	**47.28**	**23**	**35**
G.Boycott	108	193	23	246*	8114	47.72	22	42
M.A.Atherton	115	212	7	185*	7728	37.69	16	46
M.C.Cowdrey	114	188	15	182	7624	44.06	22	38
W.R.Hammond	85	140	16	336*	7249	58.45	22	24
I.R.Bell	105	181	22	235	7156	45.00	21	42
A.J.Strauss	100	178	6	177	7037	40.91	21	27

BEST TEST AVERAGES FOR ENGLAND
(Qualification: 2000 runs, ave 47.00)

	M	I	NO	HS	Runs	Ave	100	50
H.Sutcliffe	54	84	9	194	4555	60.73	16	23
K.F.Barrington	82	131	15	256	6806	58.67	20	35
W.R.Hammond	85	140	16	336*	7249	58.45	22	24
J.B.Hobbs	61	102	7	211	5410	56.94	15	28
L.Hutton	79	138	15	364	6971	56.67	19	33
D.C.S.Compton	78	131	15	278	5807	50.06	17	28
E.R.Dexter	62	102	8	205	4502	47.89	9	27
G.Boycott	108	193	23	246*	8114	47.72	22	42
E.H.Hendren	51	83	9	205*	3525	47.63	7	21
K.P.Pietersen	**104**	**181**	**8**	**227**	**8181**	**47.28**	**23**	**35**

20 TEST CENTURIES FOR ENGLAND

100s	Inns		
25	194	A.N.Cook	2006 to date
23	**181**	**K.P.Pietersen**	**2005 to 2014**
22	140	W.R.Hammond	1927 to 1947
22	188	M.C.Cowdrey	1954 to 1975
22	193	G.Boycott	1964 to 1982
21	178	A.J.Strauss	2004 to 2012
21	181	I.R.Bell	2004 to date
20	131	K.F.Barrington	1955 to 1968
20	215	G.A.Gooch	1975 to 1995

ONE-DAY INTERNATIONAL BATTING AND FIELDING AVERAGES

Opponent	M	I	NO	HS	Runs	Ave	100	50	Ct
India	28	28	3	111*	1138	45.52	1	8	6
Australia*	25	23	1	104	743	33.77	1	5	8
South Africa	17	14	4	116	646	64.60	3	2	3
Pakistan	11	11	2	130	479	53.22	2	1	2
New Zealand	11	11	1	110*	358	35.80	1	2	3
Sri Lanka	14	13	1	73	344	28.66	-	3	9
West Indies	10	9	1	100	312	39.00	1	1	2
Associates	7	6	1	59	224	44.80	-	2	2
Zimbabwe	4	3	2	77*	104	104.00	-	1	3
Bangladesh	7	5	-	23	74	14.80	-	-	1
Overall	**134**	**123**	**16**	**130**	**4422**	**41.32**	**9**	**25**	**39**

Pietersen also played two ODIs for an ICC XI v Australia in 2005-06, scoring 16 and 2.

ONE-DAY INTERNATIONAL CENTURIES

Score	Balls	Fours	Sixes	Opponent	Venue	Date
130	153	12	2	Pakistan	Dubai	2011-12
116	110	10	6	South Africa	Centurion	2004-05
111*	128	10	1	India	Cuttack	2008-09
111*	98	10	2	Pakistan	Dubai	2011-12
110*	112	8	3	New Zealand	Chester-le-Street	2008
108*	96	6	2	South Africa	Bloemfontein	2004-05
104	122	6	1	Australia	North Sound	2006-07
100*	69	7	4	South Africa	East London	2004-05
100	91	10	1	West Indies	Bridgetown	2006-07

4000 ONE-DAY INTERNATIONAL RUNS FOR ENGLAND

	M	I	NO	HS	Runs	Ave	100	50
I.R.Bell	155	151	13	141	5154	37.34	4	32
P.D.Collingwood	197	181	37	120*	5092	35.36	5	26
A.J.Stewart	170	162	14	116	4677	31.60	4	28
K.P.Pietersen	**134**	**123**	**16**	**130**	**4422**	**41.32**	**9**	**25**
M.E.Trescothick	123	122	6	137	4335	37.37	12	21
G.A.Gooch	125	122	6	142	4290	36.98	8	23
A.J.Strauss	127	126	8	158	4205	35.63	6	27
A.J.Lamb	122	118	16	118	4010	39.31	4	26

BEST ONE-DAY INTERNATIONAL AVERAGES FOR ENGLAND
(Qualification: 2000 runs, ave 38.00)

	M	I	NO	HS	Runs	Ave	100	50
I.J.L.Trott	68	65	10	137	2819	51.25	4	22
K.P.Pietersen	**134**	**123**	**16**	**130**	**4422**	**41.32**	**9**	**25**
N.V.Knight	100	100	10	125*	3637	40.41	5	25
N.H.Fairbrother	75	71	18	113	2092	39.47	1	16
A.J.Lamb	122	118	16	118	4010	39.31	4	26
R.A.Smith	71	70	8	167*	2419	39.01	4	15

BEST ONE-DAY INTERNATIONAL STRIKE RATES FOR ENGLAND
(Qualification: 2000 runs, rate 79.00)

	M	I	NO	HS	Runs	Ave	100	50	Rate
E.J.G.Morgan	112	104	19	124*	3104	36.51	6	17	89.8
A.Flintoff	138	119	16	123	3293	31.97	3	18	89.1
K.P.Pietersen	**134**	**123**	**16**	**130**	**4422**	**41.32**	**9**	**25**	**86.7**
M.E.Trescothick	123	122	6	137	4335	37.37	12	21	85.2
A.J.Strauss	127	126	8	158	4205	35.63	6	27	80.9
I.T.Botham	116	106	15	79	2113	23.21	-	9	79.1

SIX ONE-DAY INTERNATIONAL CENTURIES FOR ENGLAND

100s	Inns		
12	122	M.E.Trescothick	2000 to 2006
9	**123**	**K.P.Pietersen**	**2004 to 2013**
8	122	G.A.Gooch	1976 to 1995
7	111	D.I.Gower	1978 to 1991
6	104	E.J.G.Morgan	2009 to 2015
6	126	A.J.Strauss	2003 to 2011

TWENTY20 INTERNATIONAL BATTING AND FIELDING AVERAGES

Opponent	M	I	NO	HS	Runs	Ave	100	50	Ct
Pakistan	8	8	3	73*	348	69.60	-	4	2
India	4	4	-	53	171	42.75	-	1	-
Australia	6	6	-	47	139	23.16	-	-	5
South Africa	4	4	-	53	116	29.00	-	1	2
New Zealand	5	4	1	43	112	37.33	-	-	1
West Indies	5	5	-	31	102	20.40	-	-	1
Sri Lanka	3	3	1	42*	100	50.00	-	-	3
Zimbabwe	1	1	-	79	79	79.00	-	1	-
Ireland	1	1	-	9	9	9.00	-	-	-
Overall	**37**	**36**	**5**	**79**	**1176**	**37.93**	**-**	**7**	**14**

TWENTY20 INTERNATIONAL FIFTIES

Score	Balls	Fours	Sixes	Opponent	Venue	Date
79	37	7	4	Zimbabwe	Cape Town	2007
73*	52	8	2	Pakistan	Bridgetown	2010
62*	52	6	1	Pakistan	Abu Dhabi	2011-12
62	40	4	3	Pakistan	Dubai	2009-10
58	38	5	3	Pakistan	The Oval	2009
53	33	8	1	South Africa	Bridgetown	2010
53	39	5	3	India	Kolkata	2011-12

600 TWENTY20 INTERNATIONAL RUNS FOR ENGLAND

	M	I	NO	HS	Runs	Ave	100	50
K.P.Pietersen	37	36	5	79	1176	37.93	-	7
E.J.G.Morgan	50	49	10	85*	1147	29.41	-	6
A.D.Hales	33	33	5	116*	1062	37.92	1	7
L.J.Wright	51	45	5	99*	759	18.97	-	4
R.S.Bopara	38	35	10	65*	711	28.44	-	3

BEST TWENTY20 INTERNATIONAL AVERAGES FOR ENGLAND
(Qualification: 300 runs, ave 25.00)

	M	I	NO	HS	Runs	Ave	100	50
K.P.Pietersen	37	36	5	79	1176	37.93	-	7
A.D.Hales	33	33	5	116*	1062	36.92	1	7
E.J.G.Morgan	50	49	10	85*	1147	29.41	-	6
R.S.Bopara	38	35	10	65*	711	28.44	-	3

BEST TWENTY20 INTERNATIONAL STRIKE RATES FOR ENGLAND
(Qualification: 300 runs, rate 130.00)

	M	I	NO	HS	Runs	Ave	100	50	Rate
K.P.Pietersen	37	36	5	79	1176	37.93	-	7	141.5
A.D.Hales	33	33	5	116*	1062	36.76	1	7	138.4
L.J.Wright	51	45	5	99*	759	18.97	-	4	137.0
M.J.Lumb	27	27	1	63	552	21.23	-	3	133.6
E.J.G.Morgan	50	49	10	85*	1147	29.41	-	6	131.9
J.C.Buttler	37	31	7	67	516	21.50	-	2	131.9

10,000 INTERNATIONAL RUNS FOR ENGLAND
(Includes Test matches, one-day internationals
and Twenty20 internationals)

	M	I	NO	HS	Runs	Ave	100	50
K.P.Pietersen	**275**	**340**	**29**	**227**	**13779**	**44.30**	**32**	**67**
G.A.Gooch	243	337	12	333	13190	40.58	28	69
A.J.Stewart	303	397	35	190	13140	36.29	19	73
I.R.Bell	268	340	36	235	12498	41.11	25	75
D.I.Gower	231	315	26	215	11401	39.44	25	51
A.J.Strauss	231	308	14	177	11315	38.48	27	54
A.N.Cook	205	290	15	294	11688	42.50	30	57
M.E.Trescothick	202	268	16	219	10326	40.97	26	52

IPL CAREER

	M	I	NO	HS	Runs	Ave	100	50	Contract*
RC Bangalore (2009)	6	6	-	37	83	13.83	-	-	$1.55m
RC Bangalore (2010)	7	7	3	66*	236	59.00	-	2	$1.55m
Deccan Chargers (2011)	Did not play due to hernia injury								$0.65m
Delhi Daredevils (2012)	8	8	3	103*	269	53.80	1	1	$2.0m
Delhi Daredevils (2013)	Did not play due to knee injury								$2.0m
Delhi Daredevils (2014)	11	11	1	58	294	29.40	-	1	$1.45m
Sunrisers Hyderabad (2015)									$0.32m

* Contract sums are for a full season only; Pietersen was paid a proportion of the full amount if he was not available for every game

SOURCES

BOOKS

Anderson, James, *Jimmy: My Story* (Simon & Schuster, 2012)

Gower, David, *An Endangered Species* (Simon & Schuster, 2013)

James, Steve, *The Plan: How Fletcher and Flower Transformed English Cricket* (Bantam, 2012)

Pietersen, Kevin, *Crossing the Boundary* (Ebury, 2006)

Swann, Graeme, *The Breaks are Off: My Autobiography* (Hodder & Stoughton, 2011)

Vaughan, Michael, *Time to Declare: My Autobiography* (Hodder & Stoughton, 2009)

Veysey, Wayne, *KP Cricket Genius?: The Biography of Kevin Pietersen* (Know the Score, 2009)

MAGAZINES, NEWSPAPERS, INTERNET

'When a Leak Becomes a Flood' by Kevin Mitchell (*Observer*, 15 June 2003)

'Streaks Ahead' by Paul Kimmage (*Sunday Times*, 6 November 2005)

'I was up at six. I've a party to go to. So what is it you want?' by Rachel Cooke (*Observer*, 1 October 2006)

'Diamond Geezer' by Robert Crampton (*The Times*, 28 October 2006)

'It's Not the Ego' by Iain O'Brien (Cricinfo website, 12 September 2012)

'Aussies Should Look Out if KP Intends to Prove He's Committed' by Andrew Strauss (*Sunday Times*, 7 July 2013)

'The Best of Pietersen' by Phil Walker (*All Out Cricket*, January 2014)

'England's Spirit had Withered and Died' by Andrew Strauss (*Sunday Times*, 9 February 2014)

'Kevin Pietersen: The Man Who Fell to Earth' by Ed Smith (*New Statesman*, 20 February 2014)

RADIO, TELEVISION, ONLINE

'Keep Calm and Smash It' video on how Pietersen plays left-arm spin, pitchvision.com/kp (February 2012)

'We Need to Talk About Kevin', broadcast on BBC Radio 5 Live, 12 September 2012

'Flintoff's Ashes Legends: Kevin Pietersen', broadcast on BBC Radio 5 Live, 2 July 2013

'Kevin Pietersen Masterclass with Ian Ward', Sky Sports Television, recorded on 8 August 2013

Paul Downton interview, *Test Match Special*, BBC Radio 5 Live Sports Extra, 22 May 2014

ACKNOWLEDGEMENTS

My thanks go to Ian Marshall, at Simon & Schuster, and David Luxton for the speed with which they helped bring about this project; to Alex Butler at the *Sunday Times* for his support; to Freddie Wilde for the selfless way he broke off from university studies to assist in research; and to Gayle, Lily and Eve for telling me to get on with it and stop making a fuss.